FASHIONING THE FUTURE
TOMORROW'S WARDROBE

SUZANNE LEE
IMAGES BY WARREN DU PREEZ AND NICK THORNTON JONES

WITH 290 ILLUSTRATIONS, 247 IN COLOUR

Thames & Hudson

This book is dedicated to Amelia Mae Yolland

First published in the United Kingdom in 2005 by Thames & Hudson Ltd,
181A High Holborn, London WC1V 7QX

www.thamesandhudson.com

© 2005 Suzanne Lee
Images by Warren du Preez and Nick Thornton Jones © 2005 Warren du Preez
and Nick Thornton Jones

Reprinted 2005

British Library Cataloguing-in-Publication Data
A catalogue record for this book is available from the British Library

ISBN-13: 978-0-500-51261-6
ISBN-10: 0-500-51261-2

Printed and bound in China by C&C Offset Printing Co., Ltd.

CONTENTS

INTRODUCTION

University College for the Creative Arts
at Epsom and Farnham

paco
rabanne
1969

Who knows what clothes will be? Maybe an aerosol used to spray the body; maybe women will be dressed in coloured gases adherent to their body, or in halos of light, changing colour with the movements of the sun or with their emotions...clothes will become transparent, and revert back into being ornaments once again, reflecting women's desires to free their body from all former restrictions to let in new possibilities...free ones, really free.

1
Rudi Gernreich
Sun visors, 1965

Fashion is about experimention. In its desire to interpret the changing Zeitgeist for each new era, fashion readily embraces novel materials and techniques. New technologies drive creativity and permit designers to innovate in previously unimagined ways.

Throughout history the design and manufacture of fashion and textiles have been closely related to scientific and industrial innovation. The sewing machine revolutionized clothing production in the nineteenth century and the discovery of nylon introduced a new world of possibilities to twentieth-century fashion. Peering into the future from the early twenty-first century, we can see radical technologies that are poised to redefine how we think about the design, manufacture and consumption of fashion. The very nature of fabric, how it is produced and constructed into a garment is being challenged. Instead of coming as a roll of cloth, future visions include garments created directly from a liquid or powder, even a series of atoms that can be re-arranged as desired. The traditional process of cut-and-sew is under threat from clothes that can be sprayed-on, grown, programmed, or constructed from *smart* textiles that respond to our individual needs.

Historically, fashion designers have not only embraced new technologies in the fabrication and fashioning of clothes, but also used the imagery of science and technology to express modernity and progress. In 1936, Elsa Schiaparelli presented fashion collections that included prints of thermometers to 'register' a wearer's passion and celebrated contemporary technologies such as the telegraph and radio. She also collaborated with industry, working with French textile producer Colombet to create a 'glass cape' from their Rhodophane material in 1934.

1
Vienna-born, California-based designer Rudi Gernreich was recognized as anticipating many trends in fashion, often years before his contempories. Featured on the cover of *Time* Magazine in December 1967, he was described as 'the most way-out, far-ahead designer in the US'.

2/3
A fighter pilot during the Second World War, the Florentine designer Emilio Pucci embraced the space age in his uniforms for Braniff International in 1965. Clear plastic bubbles were designed to protect the stewardesses' hair and, combined with the wide round collar of the coat, invite comparison with the contemporary astronaut's attire.

2
Pucci
Braniff stewardess, 1965

3
NASA
Astronaut John Glenn

Schiaparelli challenged the boundaries of fashion through her dialogue with contemporary Surrealist art, while early twentieth-century artists, particularly the Russian avant-garde and Italian Futurists, entered the realm of clothing design with radical propositions for modernist dress.

Several decades later, in the 1960s, a new generation of modernist fashion designers, including Pierre Cardin, André Courrèges, Rudi Gernreich and Paco Rabanne, were inspired by the glamour of flight, the space race and Pop Art. They experimented with new synthetics to create dynamic new shapes, styles and decoration. Idealistic, even naïve, as those designs may seem now, they represent a defining era in which fashion did not reference the past but looked to the future. Since then, the fashion world has largely returned to the relative safety of retro styling. In terms of technological innovation, it could be argued that fashion has been in stasis. Instead, sportswear has become the new arena for hi-tech clothing.

Today, high-end designer fashion is struggling to find its identity in a competitive global market. Demands on the consumer pocket are greater than ever, especially in the areas of health and beauty, personal technology, home interiors and holidays, and the amount spent on fashion is declining. In addition, social, cultural and environmental concerns such as sustainability are engaging the educated consumer. Fashion, in order to thrive long term, needs to adapt and evolve. It is technological work going on in research laboratories that promises to turn the fashion world on its head once again.

This book anticipates a future shaped by new materials and technologies that present exciting creative possibilities for fashion. The integration of electronics into

4
A *Punch* forecast for 1907, this cartoon depicts a woman and a man each with an antenna embedded in their hats receiving, respectively, an amatory message and the racing results.

5
Widely acknowledged as the 'father' of wearable computing, Steve Mann's experiments over the years have been influential in the field of 'wearables' and augmented-reality research. His early wearables were bulky, heavy components bolted to helmets, strapped on with belts and carried in backpacks. Over the years, with electronic miniaturization, Mann's wearable system has become streamlined – gone is the radio antenna on his head and the head-mounted display has shrunk to be concealed behind dark glasses.

1980	Early 1990s

Mid-1990s	Late 1990s

4
Punch
Wireless telegraphy, 1906

5
Steve Mann
Wearable computing, 1980–late 1990s

cloth for example, promises evening wear that changes colour based on mood, dresses that subtly change shape, and coats that display downloadable designs. Until now, electric fashion existed only in science fiction, but as the enabling technologies begin to emerge from laboratories so these fictions become fact. Far from the runway, researchers at the intersection of *materials science*, electrical engineering, chemistry and *biotechnology* are designing the foundations for the haute-tech couture world of tomorrow.

Initial markets to benefit from these new textile and clothing products will be the lucrative military, medical, sport and well-being industries, where performance equals efficiency and the benefits are obvious. Inevitably, however, these new technologies will eventually filter down to the fashion market, and when they do, future generations of designers will have a new set of tools to work with, potentially changing fashion forever. The implications are phenomenal for designers, producers, global brands and consumers alike.

This book considers the future frontiers of fashion and technology and, for the first time, brings this research out of laboratories and academia and into the fashion world. *Fashioning the Future* aims to provide an inspirational guide to tomorrow's wardrobe. Each chapter opens with a fashion 'dreamscape', an imaginative visual exploration of its themes. These images were produced especially for this book in collaboration with the leading British image-makers, Warren du Preez and Nick Thornton Jones. A new technological landscape emerges, mapping the development of *electro-textiles* and smart fibres through to biotechnology and *nanotechnology*. The futuristic chapter titles guide the reader through an imaginary

6
Steven Lisberger's 1982 ground-breaking science-fiction movie *Tron*, starring Jeff Bridges, created a world inside the computer. Projections of future clothing took the form of glowing electric bodysuits.

7/8
London-based designer Hamish Morrow collaborated with United Visual Artists (UVA), known for their stadium projections for pop bands such as Massive Attack, and image-makers Warren du Preez and Nick Thornton Jones to create a series of 'Virtual Print' dresses for his Spring/Summer 2004 show. Models stood still as their dresses were painted with transient light patterns. Later, these 'moments' were captured and digitally printed onto a series of limited-edition dresses.

6
Tron
Glowing costumes, 1982

7
Hamish Morrow
Spring/Summer 2004

8
Hamish Morrow
Spring/Summer 2004

wardrobe and are a distillation of the discussion of each technology. In many cases the technologies overlap, so that we may, for example, expect a future garment to be simultaneously programmable, glowing and shape-changing.

When will we start seeing these radical new visions? As with any future-gazing, it is hard to say for sure; some are already here, others may not emerge for another five, ten, fifty or even one hundred years. In some instances, significant ethical concerns may need to be resolved; some technologies may never come to fruition. It is interesting to note that the motivation most designers cite for harnessing technology in fashion is purely to further the creative process, to achieve something in a new way. In contrast, science and technology researchers are often looking for an application for a particular discovery. One thing is certain, where fashion is concerned, the use of technology for technology's sake will only result in gimmickry.

Where most discussion of technology in fashion relates to the technical aspects of production, *Fashioning the Future* examines how new technologies might be creative tools for fashion design. This book aims to address the technophobia of those working in high fashion and to enlighten technologists about the motivations of fashion designers. It envisions fashion created by hi-tech artisans in techno-ateliers. It is true that comfort, practicality, performance, and the expression of status and fantasy, are just as important in dress today as they have ever been, but although clothing can perform useful functions, at the heart of fashion lies escapism. For haute-tech fashion to become part of our lives, it will have to transcend functionality, be invisible, intuitive, and enhance our experiences. This cannot be achieved without the creative engagement of fashion designers – technology is nothing without craft.

9

In 2003, Tribe Art, an arts organization funded by Formula 1's B.A.R. Team Honda, comissioned British-based, conceptual fashion designer Hussein Chalayan to produce a film. *Place to Passage* featured a lone girl seated in a futuristic pod speeding into a future/past through memories of moments and places from London to Istanbul. Here, as in all his work, Chalayan's aesthetic reflects his interests in hi-tech aviation and car design, mixing the utopian futurism of science fiction with complex cultural observations about political and geographical boundaries, as reflected in his native Cyprus.

9
Hussein Chalayan
Place to Passage, 2003

CHAPTER ONE /
THE SPRAY-ON DRESS

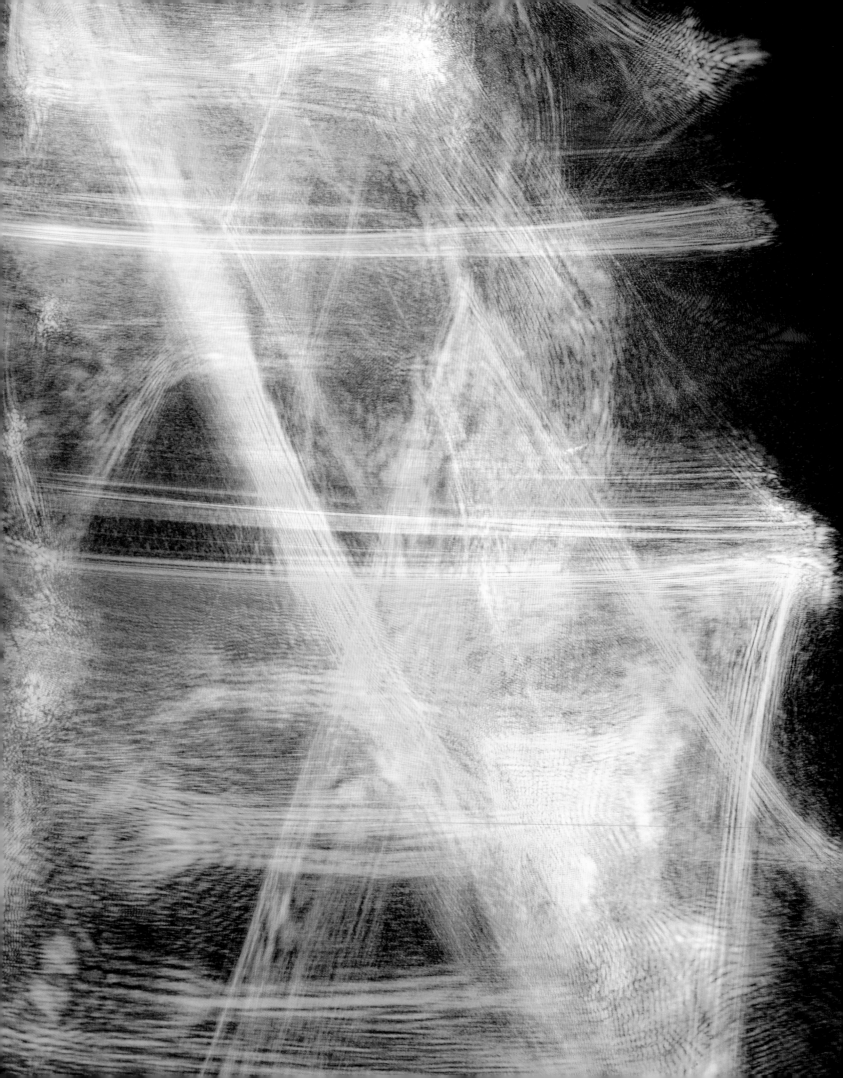

rudi gernreich 1971

Once the sewing machine has been replaced or sophisticated, once a designer can spray-on clothes or transmigrate fabrics to the body, new things will happen…The designer will become less artist, more technician. He'll be like an architect or engineer, with a sound background in chemistry.

It was over three decades ago that the futuristic American designer Rudi Gernreich predicted the demise of fashion design as we know it. He would no doubt have approved of the unique creative path being pursued by London-based fashion designer Manel Torres. Forget sewing machines, rolls of cloth, pattern-cutting – and designers. If Manel Torres has his way, clothes will come from a can.

A dress created with an aerosol? What started out as a dream for Torres is about to become a reality. His company FabriCan has literally created fabric in a can. The aerosol doesn't actually contain a dress or indeed a garment of any kind, but it does hold enough 'spray-on non-woven fabric' to create an item of clothing on the body. The user simply sprays 'cloth' where needed. What looks like an ordinary aerosol discharges a fine, fibrous cloud that adheres to the skin's surface, creating a non-woven body-covering. This is fashion without the need for patterns and toiles or seams and fastenings. If a specific shoulder shape, collar or sleeve detail is desired, a cardboard or plastic guide mould can be created to provide a three-dimensional structure on which to spray. This would be removed once the required shape and rigidity were achieved. With spray-on fabric all the conventions of garment construction would become obsolete. Clothing created this way would most probably be disposable, although if the wearer wanted to peel or cut-off a garment it might be worn again by sealing up the opening with a little more spray-on cloth. Imagine those heavy suitcases lugged on vacation replaced by a few atomisers in a handbag.

...the couture laboratory

Seamless fashion is not exactly new. Some of the more innovative fashion designers of the twentieth century experimented with moulded and pre-formed clothes. During

10/13

Fashion designer Manel Torres experimenting in his laboratory at Imperial College, London. Test tubes and pressurized spraying equipment replace fabrics and sewing machines.

10/13

Manel Torres

Fashioning chemistry, 2004

11

12

13

the late 1960s both the Spanish fashion-designer Paco Rabanne and the French designer Pierre Cardin advocated the modernization of couture. Following his use of materials such as metal, paper and plastic in his collection of July 1968, Paco Rabanne showed an outfit that was entirely moulded: no stitching or seaming. Named Giffo, it was a collaboration with Louis Giffard, a synthetic products manufacturer, and was made by spraying a 'cloud of plastic into a mould'.[1] The technique, which enabled garments to be made at a speed and cost previously unimaginable, was duly patented. 'One raincoat, complete with pockets and buttons, could be produced per minute.'[2]

The same year that Rabanne showed his revolutionary moulded Giffo clothes, Pierre Cardin launched his Cardines. These were pre-formed dresses with a decorative three-dimensional surface pattern made from his patented Cardine fabric, a synthetic cloth, Dynel, manufactured by Union Carbide. Again, this was a groundbreaking procedure that did away with cut-and-sew techniques to create instant fashion. Both approaches challenged traditional methods of garment manufacturing, but were clearly too ahead of their time to be appropriated by the mainstream. Current thinking on recycling and sustainability, however, encourages the use of one material or fibre for a whole garment[3] and so perhaps these early investigations into mouldable fashion have come of age.

Contemporary fashion production offers various alternatives to cut-and-sew. Ultrasonic welding enables construction without the need for sewing machines or thread and we now have three-dimensional knitting machines, designed by companies like Shima-Seiki, whose 'WholeGarment' technology can produce clothes with no seams at all. Issey Miyake, a pioneer in the world of fashion and technology, is

28

14
Artist-in-residence Vere Smith painted unique designs onto clothing for customers at Take 6 boutique on London's Carnaby Street in the 1960s.

15
This one-piece swimsuit with bra section was made of two foam-rubber discs held on by suction.

16
Pierre Cardin's belief is that 'Haute Couture is a creative laboratory where forms and volumes can be studied. The immensity of the universe and microscopy of the cell, computers and geometry: these are the sources of my inspiration. The garments I prefer are those I create for tomorrow's world.'

17
In 1969, the Spanish fashion designer Paco Rabanne stated 'I am only interested in the research for new, contemporary materials.' For Rabanne, new materials challenged traditional forms of construction and led to the creation of new shapes.

14
Vere Smith
Take 6 boutique, 1969

15
Ruben Torres
Concord bikini, 1967

16
Pierre Cardin
Cardine dress, 1968

17
Paco Rabanne
Giffo dress, 1968

more than a designer of clothes: Miyake is a designer of clothes-making processes. He leads the vanguard with his A-POC (A Piece of Cloth) line: a clothing system whereby a single thread enters a computerized machine and a finished, but customizable, garment emerges at the other end. Miyake describes his creative journey as a search for 'a state of clothing that reflects its time and lifestyle'.[4] A-POC proposes a radical rethink of fashion manufacture for the twenty-first century.

Spanish fashion-designer Manel Torres confesses he has always been obsessed with the distant future. He studied at the Royal College of Art in London, basing his MA womenswear collection of 1997 on a forecast for 2050, and investigating the concept of spray-on fabric for his doctorate. During his research Torres found that scientists were attracted by the way he approached fashion, engaging easily with his ideas, and on completing his PhD he moved to Imperial College, London, which specializes in science and technology. While there he created FabriCan and now holds a worldwide patent for spray-on fabric. When asked about the leap from studying art and design to chemistry, he is obviously not fazed:

The good thing about chemistry is that there are always books for answers. In fashion we don't have answers, only more questions. In science you can find out if this polymer will dissolve in this liquid. As artists and designers we make one thing, for example a painting, and it's impossible to reproduce exactly the same again. But in science, because they measure everything and follow a strict methodology, they can reproduce the same results over and over. I learnt this the hard way. At first I was working in the lab spontaneously as a creative person would; I would create something amazing but be unable to recall how I did it. I didn't keep notes as I went along and so I lost the recipe. Now I keep detailed records![5]

18/19
Issey Miyake's revolutionary A-POC (A Piece of Cloth) line is a play on epoch and the idea of clothing that evolves from one era to the next. The hi-tech seamless knitting machinery used in A-POC production produces a tube of fabric that contains an entire outfit, ready to be cut out by the wearer. The sophisticated construction even allows variable shapes and lengths from the same designed section. A garment starts and ends as the wearer chooses, encouraging the customer to take part in the final design process.

20
This stitchless, seamless, welded and molded dress in polyester jersey was one of a run of experimental garments in which Hamish Morrow used different techniques to produce clothing with no stitching. The lack of seams was due to clever cutting that facilitated a wrap-around shape. The edges were finished with thermo-plastic film to prevent fraying and stretching, the bust shaping was achieved with cold-molding over a breast form, and the transparent straps were applied with a sonic welder.

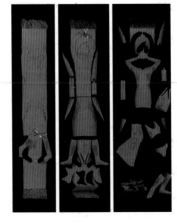

18
Issey Miyake A-POC
King & Queen, Spring/Summer 1999

19
Issey Miyake A-POC
Baguette, Spring/Summer 2000

20
Hamish Morrow
Spring/Summer 2004

The FabriCan spray formulation consists of fibres mixed with a binder. Early prototypes used cotton fibres to create a delicate web of cloth that had a slightly powdery feel, however Torres is confident that almost any fibre could be used: 'It's more a question of finding suppliers who can deliver the raw ingredient in an appropriate form.'[6] Imagine spray-on silk, wool or gossamer-thin cashmere.

Since the fibres are being delivered in a diffused form all manner of extras could be added, from glitter effects to perfume and even drug treatments. Spraying fibres allows for the control of thickness and density, creating a layered cloth that might waft as light as mist in one area but provide firm protection in another. One sample Torres demonstrates already incorporates a high level of elasticity to enable stretch. Olympic swimmers of the future may be armed with a small can of elastic fibre minimally sprayed to protect their modesty. This is fabric that can be applied on demand. Multiple cans could produce complex layers of colour, and intricate three-dimensional shapes, which would be impossible to create in a woven cloth, could be generated with ease. Torres is keen to ensure the whole product is as environmentally friendly as possible; the material is biodegradable and the cans recyclable.

...fashion as chemical formula

With 'spray-on fashion' rapid changes in trends could be obtained simply by tweaking the product's chemical formula, and previously unimagined fashions could be created. A designer might present a collection of clothes in seasonal colours and fragrances: 'This season I shall be wearing mostly vanilla.'

Spray-on fabric is such a creatively liberating concept that there appears no end to possible applications. This, unusually, is an invention inspired by fashion but it could

21/22
Supplied as a DIY kit, Betsey Johnson's 1966 'instant' fashion consisted of a plastic shell in a choice of four colours to which the wearer could add stick-on cut-outs. Shapes such as stars and petals were positioned to cover as much or as little as the wearer desired.

23
In the late 1960s disposable paper clothing was an instant success as wearable Pop Art. It was started by the Scott Paper Company in 1966, which used a material called Duraweve for dresses that acted as advertising billboards. Not long after, paper-like garments were made using DuPont's Tyvek, a non-woven material that could be washed several times. Paper dresses were printed with pop imagery but were not meant to last long. In the same way that Pop Art referenced consumer culture so fashion copied supermarket packaging – the New York label Wippette created a nylon jersey canned dress.

21
Betsey Johnson
Stick-on fashion, Spring 1966

22
Betsey Johnson -
Stick-on fashion, Spring 1966

23
Wippette
Canned Dress, 1966

be applied to anything, from the upholstery of a chair to the skin of an aircraft. Surfaces could be re-made at will; you could peel off the existing colour, texture or scent and apply a new one. Fashion already has considerable influence on interior design, and spray-on fabric would allow for instant makeovers at a fraction of the cost of buying new furniture.

In fact, spray-on fabric is so easy to apply that it is ripe for abuse by consumers, or even by companies as an extreme form of guerrilla marketing. Torres has already envisaged its use by brands to 'colonize' other products; basic consumables such as a bottle of mineral water might acquire a new identity. Fashion, already ephemeral, could be applied one second and removed the next. In the future we may see brands becoming no more than 'liquid packaging'. Is it such a leap of imagination to consider the disappearance of a brand as a physical product and for it to take on a spray-on identity instead? So, a luxury-goods house need not be involved in the expensive business of manufacturing products, but could make just exclusive cans of logo. Customers would be able to apply this to whatever they wish; branding taken to its zenith where marketing, advertising and product are one and the same. Applying the brand may be achievable using a dual can: reservoir A storing a base coat, reservoir B the logo colour, and the lid equipped with a special stencil-shaped nozzle to create the logo itself. In an instant you would have a Louis Vuitton laptop or a Gucci sofa.

Torres also sees his product making its way into the medical and healthcare industry. A textile in a can could provide a sterilized, biodegradable and instant covering for wounds, and could be used at the scene of an accident or in a war zone. This cloth might have additional benefits, such as treating the wound or even alerting a patient

33

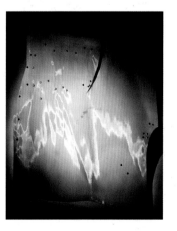

24
Issey Miyake
Colombe, Spring/Summer 1991

25
Issey Miyake
Colombe, Spring/Summer 1991

when it is safe for it to be removed. We are likely to see 'well-being' products with fashion appeal: spray-on Burberry bandages could be sold at a premium.

We are now witnessing a move towards the convergence of fashion, cosmetics, health and medical products into new textile hybrids: 'fabriceuticals' (fabrics with pharmaceutical qualities), 'cosmeceuticals' (cosmetics with pharmaceutical qualities) and cosmetics that parade as clothing. These trends may also be indicative of how fashion products and technology will evolve in the future. With apparel sales in long-term decline but cosmetic and well-being markets growing at a vertiginous rate, fashion may find that entirely new product opportunities exist in the crossover potential of these industries. Torres observes that for our ageing and image-obsessed western society, body-maintenance may take financial priority over fashion.

Torres's vision of the fashion house of the future is one where he recruits people from diverse backgrounds, not just fashion, to create a cross-discipline mix of designers and scientists working together. He believes this would be key: such a team would 'create better designs because they are bringing [a] fresh perspective and expertise to fashion'.[7] Indeed, maybe 'fashion house' is no longer an appropriate term. The reality may be closer to a creative laboratory.

…designer-in-residence

The in-store experience might take different forms when spray-on clothes are being retailed. The first option would be as simple as customers purchasing the product to take home to create an outfit or garment for themselves. Fashion retailing in the twenty-first century is increasingly about entertainment or 'retailment' and 'mass-customization'. Stores might replace sales assistants with a premium service whereby

26/27
Electrospinning is a technique that has been around since the 1930s but it is receiving renewed interest from researchers investigating the application of technology to the clothing industry. The process uses an electrostatic charge to disperse a jet of polymer into a fine non-woven fabric. At the US Army Soldier Systems Center in Natick, Massachusetts, scientists are assessing the viability of manufacturing seamless 'couture' military uniforms from 3D body-scanned data.

34

26
US Army Soldier Systems Center
Close-up of electrospun fibres

27
US Army Soldier Systems Center
Electrospinning simulation on 3D bodyform

an artist or designer-in-residence, working in a luxurious, exclusive salon, would create an on-the-spot spray-on outfit. A haute-couture line might consist of a new series of chemical formulae in limited editions. Special colours, textures, patterns and scents could be created. For a jewelled effect, one can imagine adding silver, gold, diamond or ruby dust to the mix. A client might commission the 'designer-chemist' to make a one-off formulation for a wedding dress – a delicate lace that can be peeled off the bride on her wedding night.

Gernreich's prediction that future fashion designers will be more akin to chemists than artists remains contentious. It took artistic vision to imagine spray-on clothing and in all likelihood it will be creative designers who push the scientific boundaries of this invention. As Torres enthuses:

At the moment it's just fun thinking about all the possibilities. What I'm most pleased about is having been able to hold onto the original idea and to make it a reality. Spray-on fabric will be limited only by the imagination of the people using it.[8]

28/31
The naked model is sprayed with Manel Torres's FabriCan – a fine mist of coloured cotton fibre that builds up layers as and where required. Once a fibre layer is established, it can remain as a second skin or be peeled back to create volume and drape. Additional details and features can be integrated by placing extra cloth or decoration on the body and spraying over the top to keep them in place.

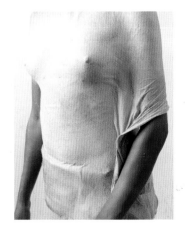

28/31 Manel Torres
FabriCan garment experiments, 2004

29

30

31

CHAPTER TWO /
THE PROGRAMMABLE JACKET

neil gershenfeld 1999

It's not too far...to see wearable computers as a new step in our evolution as a species. The organization of life has been defined by communications. It was a big advance for molecules to work together to form cells, for cells to work together to form animals, for animals to work together to form families, and for families to work together to form communities. Each of these steps, clearly part of the evolution of life, conferred important benefits that were of value to the species. Moving computing into clothing opens a new era in how we interact with each other, the defining characteristic of what it means to be human.

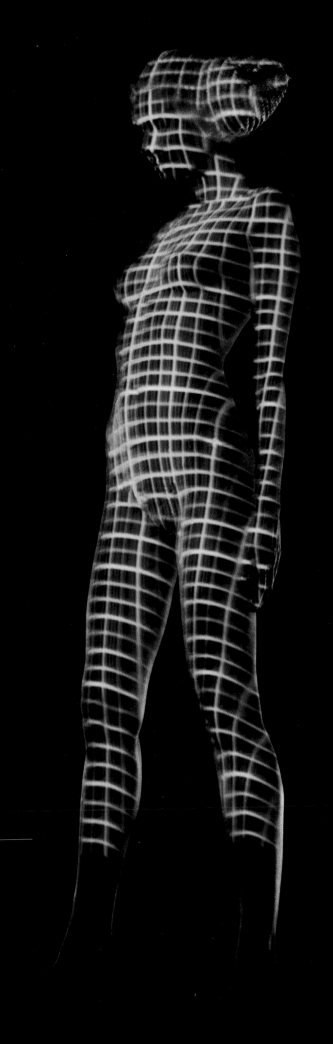

'Smart clothing', 'wearables' and 'wearable computing' are somewhat equivocal terms describing a genre of clothing that functions at a whole new level – electronic. Capable of processing information on the moving body, this field stems from computing research begun in the late 1960s,[1] but which gained momentum with the miniaturization of components in the 1980s and 1990s. Steve Mann, an early pioneer of wearable computing at MIT (Massachusetts Institute of Technology in Cambridge, Massachusetts), and subsequently at the University of Toronto, paved the way for a generation of researchers keen to transform elements of the personal desktop computer into something that could be worn and operated on the body. This has, until very recently, been a geeky, male-dominated area of research located in various university computing departments. Most funding comes from the military, for whom wearable information processing for soldiers to use in the field is highly desirable.

The term 'wearables' generally relates to hard computing components that clip onto belts or that are worn around the body in pockets or slings. They are mobile, task-oriented work accessories used by operatives in the field who require information at their fingertips. Despite the name, wearables aren't really wearable. Reminiscent of James Cameron's *Terminator*,[2] wearable computers often feature a digital display over the eye that superimposes virtual information onto the user's view of reality. This is known as *augmented reality*.

Since the 1970s, efforts have been focused on taking the electronics housed within a computer and finding ways to distribute them around the body as efficiently as possible, while solving problems of viewing data, interface design, connectivity, powering and so forth. This has led to a cyborg aesthetic that has little to do with clothing and nothing to do with fashion. It could be described as a top-down

Foster-Miller, a company that specializes in electro-textiles, worked with the US Army to integrate data and communication antennas into a soldier's uniform. The antenna is strategically looped around the body ensuring no interference or loss of operation. A textile antenna is one of the essential components of wearable electronics and computing.

34
General Dynamics' Eagle Enterprise unit, a supplier to the US Army's Objective Force Warrior (OFW) program, is designing a soldier ensemble intended for use by 2010. The OFW program wants to create a 'networked soldier' using a uniform that combines head-to-toe individual protection with netted communication, supplied by soldier-worn power sources. The uniform would also monitor heart rate and respiration, and the helmets would receive real-time video from overhead drones. The US Army's goal is the creation of a 'digital battlefield' where soldiers, tanks and drones are connected by a common network in which the soldier is a 'node'.

35
Founded in 1990, Xybernaut is a manufacturer of wearable computer hardware and related software for those who need maximum mobility and portability. The voice-activated processor and head-mounted colour display (HMD) can allow workers hands-free access to information.

32
US Army Soldier Systems Center
Wearable electronic network

33
Foster-Miller
Textile antenna

34
US Army
Objective Force Warrior (OFW)

35
Xybernaut
Wearable computer

approach – 'let's put computers into clothing' (hardware/wear). Contemporary research efforts, however, have seen the limitations in this method, such as the lack of comfort, washability and user-friendliness, and are now coming at the problem from a bottom-up direction – 'let's make the cloth itself compute' (software/wear). The future may prove both approaches to be right, with two very different products emerging. One is worn as an accessory with a hi-tech spec for work-led applications, while the other, a textile-based solution, serves much more everyday purposes, becoming a literal part of the fabric of our lives.

36/37

An early example of wearable computing consisted of a computer that fitted inside a shoe. This small apparatus could be used covertly in a casino to time the ball on a spinning roulette table. A footswitch and wireless transfer enabled a prediction of where the ball would land to pass from the observer's shoe to that of the accomplice placing the bets. The Eudaemons were a group of researchers in the physics department at the University of California, Santa Cruz (UCSC).

...from portable to wearable

But why would we want to embed electronics into our clothes? The average twenty-first century commuter might carry any combination of, or all of, the following: mobile phone, PDA (personal digital assistant), MP3 player, digital camera and laptop. Anticipating a backlash from the technology-laden consumer, manufacturers have started to consider new ways of accommodating portable products.

Electronic devices have become miniaturized, along with components, to the point where people have reached the limit on the size of interface with which they are comfortable. This means making ever-smaller products is not really an option. One solution is to create a single device that might perform multi-functions (phone, camera, MP3 and PDA), but while this is forging ahead other concerns have emerged. How might we make someone's experience of technology more intuitive, less invasive, more human-centric? These questions have fuelled developments in creative disciplines such as textiles, architecture, interaction design, dance and performance, where practitioners probe how we might interact with technology in new, more empowering ways.

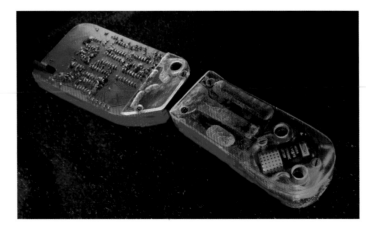 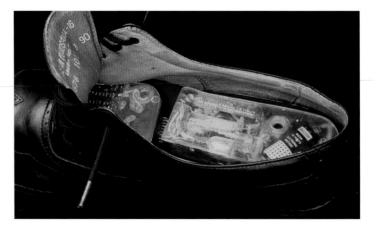

36/37
The Eudaemons
Digital shoe computer, 1978

37

In 1988, Mark Weiser, then head of the Computer Science Laboratory at Xerox PARC (Palo Alto Research Center), invented the term *ubiquitous computing* to describe a future where invisible computers would be embedded in everyday objects:

The most profound technologies are those that disappear. They weave themselves into the fabric of everyday life until they are indistinguishable from it.[3]

The pursuit of pervasive computing is described by electronics giant Philips as *ambient intelligence*. At its HomeLab research facility at Eindhoven, The Netherlands, Philips is exploring how we might live, work and play in the future and where *smart* clothing might fit into the picture. *Wireless* and *Bluetooth* technologies enable devices to communicate with one another without being physically connected – no need for cables. On walking through a door a lapel badge on a coat might 'recognize' the wearer and turn on the lights, hi-fi, even the kettle, according to habit. Clothing and accessories might become part of a smart environment that can be tailored to an individual's requirements, all operating autonomously via radio waves. In 2000, Philips published a book entitled *New Nomads* which mapped out the company's vision for wearable electronics. The discussion centred on the revolutionary convergence of two disparate industries – fashion and electronics. Contrary to much prior research, which had tried to force technology onto clothing, often with awkward results, Philips recognized the need to understand and work with fashion design. According to the CEO of Philips Design, Stefano Marzano:

What we are talking about here is a new lifestyle and business revolution – one that will require the electronics industry to 'think emotionally'. To guarantee

38
These Puma running shoes were affixed with a small computer that counted time and distance, and this information was then downloaded onto an Apple II computer using the game port.

39
In American *Vogue*'s February 1939 issue, which celebrated the New York World's Fair, leading industrial designers were asked for their predictions of future fashion. Designer Gilbert Rohde prophesied the man of the next century would be wearing an air-conditioned Solosuit, an all-in-one outfit that zipped on and off. An antenna hat 'snatches radio and Omega waves out of the ether', receiving and transmitting as required. 'Featherweight equipment, carried in a belt, transforms the Omega waves to warm or cool the body through a network of hair-like wires woven into a cloth of synthetic yarn, providing man with an air-conditioned garment.'

38
Puma
RS computer shoe, mid-1980s

39
Gilbert Rohde
Solosuit, 1939

human-focused solutions, we cannot expect the fashion industry to adapt itself to technology. Rather, the technology industry will have to learn how to deal with fashion.[4]

...electro-textiles

It would not be the first time that technology took the lead from the fashion industry. In 1834 Charles Babbage, often referred to as 'the father of modern computing', was inspired by the first loom to weave patterns automatically when he conceived the idea for an Analytical Engine. Although never built, this had many of the logical features of the present-day computer. Babbage realized that the holes in the punched-card system used to operate Joseph Marie Jacquard's textile loom were the perfect binary system for his calculating machine. Ada Lovelace, Lord Byron's daughter, who worked with Babbage, said that 'the Analytical Engine weaves algebraic patterns just as the Jacquard loom weaves flowers and leaves.'[5]

Now, in the twenty-first century, humble cloth is once again paving the way for the next generation of information processing, except this time the fabric and electronics have become one. In the nascent field of *electro-textiles* (e-textiles), it is fibres, yarns, ribbons and fabrics that can conduct electricity. These fabrics can sense when and how they are being touched, acting as sensors, switches, transistors, power cables, antennae and displays. Traditional fashion and textile techniques, such as coating, printing, embroidery, appliqué, quilting, weaving and knitting, can create conductive fabrics and clothing using carbon, stainless steel, silver, and even gold. Thus baroque gold embroidery might become a switch,[6] a decorative Jacquard might receive a radio signal,[7] and a handknit cardigan might sense poor posture.[8]

46

40
Petra Spee's concept for a sports jacket makes a feature of the electronic conductive ribbons that connect a textile-control panel on the sleeve to the MP3 player module. Infineon Technologies is a German chip manufacturer that is integrating microelectronics into textiles.

41
As part of their New Nomads project, Philips wearable electronics team forecast 'Imaginair (2000)' – an air hostess's uniform incorporating a personal digital assistant with flexible LCD screen, wireless earpiece and microphone.

42
'L'écharpe communicante', or communicating scarf, is part of a concept for business travellers consisting of a jacket and scarf that house a computer touch screen, microprocessor, keyboard, phone and camera. The wearer could connect to the Internet, send e-mails, access files or watch a film. A microphone, two earphones hidden in the collar, and a webcam complete the system, enabling the user to speak to others, organize video conferences and send photos. The 'écharpe communicante' was a joint project by France Télécom's R&D Studio Créatif, Naziha Mestaoui and Yacine Aït Kaci of the hybrid-design company Electronic Shadow, and the fashion designer Christophe Beaufays.

40
Infineon Technologies
MP3 player jacket, 2002

41
Philips
Wired air hostess, 2000

42
France Télécom
Communicating scarf, 2000

The electronic nature of a garment might be acknowledged, becoming part of the design, or it can be completely concealed. E-textiles underpin many of the new concepts for clothing explored throughout this book.

...data-suits and body-networks

Clothing is an inescapable fact of life. While some understand it as part of an individual's self-expression and embrace it for its aesthetic qualities, others see its purpose as more practical or functional. Those who choose their clothing according to its performance are most likely to find electronic clothing appealing. Integrated electronic functions might be attractive to people who require access to information on the move, such as businesspeople, medics, sportsmen and women, and the police. A garment might become a central 'hub' to other portable technologies, linking personal devices such as phones as well as making connections to the external environment. A discrete button on the cuff of a 'data-suit' might light up to notify someone in a meeting that they have a message, even possibly displaying it. A uniform might be programmed to give security access to certain zones in a building, opening doors as an authorized person approaches.

In 1995, at MIT's Media Lab, Thomas Zimmerman and Neil Gershenfeld came up with the idea of using the electrical conductivity of the body itself to send data or signals to another person or device. This so-called *personal area network* (PAN), created with the aid of a small computer concealed, for example, in a shoe, sends harmless electrical signals through the body. So, with a handshake two people can exhange digital business cards between their shoe computers, or simply by putting a hand on a doorknob it can be unlocked.[9] Any device we carry around can potentially act as a PAN device: watch, mobile phone or even credit card.

43/45
Textile artist Frances Geesin works with synthetic materials that she electroplates. Although initially her use of electroplating was for aesthetic effect, Geesin discovered it had the added function of lending conductivity to yarn. She became an early pioneer of electro-textiles, working as a consultant to BASF and Philips in the mid-1990s. She has since collaborated with her partner Ron Geesin, a sound artist, to produce interactive textile works that use cloth to control sound and light. Their work has been exhibited at London's Science Museum.

46
The UK company Eleksen is a pioneer of conductive fabric sensing and switching applications. Its core technology ElekTex incorporates fabric sensors with electronics and software. An ElekTex sensor can detect where it is being pressed and to a degree how hard it is being pressed. Among the company's products is a fabric QWERTY keyboard which can be rolled up when not in use and is designed for people on the move. Eleksen's fabric keyboard for the Logitech M500 PDA range, pictured here, received the IDEA Business Week Gold Award for Innovation (2004).

48

43
Frances Geesin
Electroplated hands, 2000

44
Frances Geesin
Sensory fabric, 1994

45
Frances Geesin
Electro-textile keyboard, 1994

46
Eleksen
Logitech keyboard, 2000

This may sound extreme to many but not to Microsoft, who in June 2004 patented the human body as a computer network.[10] The full patent describes the ability to use the body not only as a conduit but also as a surface. So, for example, we might type on our skin. The term PAN is now widely used to describe a network on and around the body, i.e. linking up a series of mobile devices using Bluetooth or *infrared* technology. Instead of using a person's body to transfer data, their clothing could perform this task. Embedding electronics into clothing offers new ways of using technology. Apart from entering information by typing, a fabric interface might be pulled, twisted, stretched or stroked.

Since Zimmerman and Gershenfeld first outlined the idea of a PAN, others, somewhat confusingly, have coined the term BAN or *body area network*. This concept is being developed by the medical industry for wirelessly connecting implanted medical devices and on-body sensors with a bedside transceiver. Data is then forwarded via a mobile phone or the Internet to a doctor or other hospital staff. With a two-way link, doctors can remotely control and adjust an implanted device.

...power dressing

Leaving aside the not insignificant issues of wear and washability, a significant stumbling block to the advancement of electro-textiles is likely to be a viable power source. Power is not a concern that has bothered fashion designers in the past, but how to power clothing effectively has now become a critical issue. To date, size, weight and battery life have been fundamental obstacles in the proliferation of wearable technologies. The power issue has been slow to seek a fabric solution. Existing types of battery, used in consumer electronics, have been pocketed or strapped to the body, but this is unsatisfactory for clothing. One possible system

47
An early experiment in the integration of computing with clothing is this Levi's denim jacket adapted to become a musical instrument, developed at MIT's Media Lab. The embroidered keypad over the left pocket is sewn with mildly conductive thread that, when touched, sends a signal to another processor, which in turn runs a MIDI synthesizer. Sound is projected through mini-speakers in the jacket's pockets and the system is battery powered.

48
The MIThril project was established by researchers at MIT's Media Lab with the aim of developing and prototyping wearable computing. They want to support people in their daily lives by building technology that is reliable, comfortable, useful, and maximizes the time of the person wearing it. The MIThril hardware combines body-worn computation, sensing and networking in a clothing-integrated design.

49
KnoWear have designed this prototype for a wireless interactive gaming suit. Each garment would be tailored to the individual using 3D bodyscans, and configured with personal technology preferences. Worn as an undergarment that wirelessly connects to the Internet, TechnoLust would let the wearer play virtual games from any location. On encountering another participant, a game of electronic caresses could begin with pulses sent back and forth electronically.

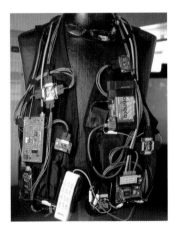

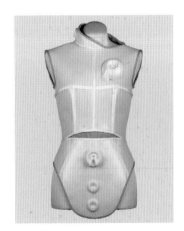

47
MIT Media Laboratory
Musical jacket, 1997

48
MIT Media Laboratory
MIThril vest 1000

49
KnoWear
TechnoLust, 2000

might be to hang your jacket on an overnight 'charger-hanger' – an electric clotheshorse that recharges clothes for the next day's wear.

The practicality of powering smart clothing has prompted researchers to explore various possibilities based on the potential offered by the human body itself. Proposals include: harvesting the heat differential between the body's surface and the garment;[11] kinetic power produced by walking that could be taken from a shoe;[12] harnessing static electricity; or using the body's large surface area to capture and store solar power within fabric. *Photovoltaic* (solar-powered) fabric could mean an entire garment becomes a battery capable of powering electronic functions within itself. Future fabrics may be woven from *polymer* fibres manipulated on a molecular level to capture light and turn it into electricity.

                    ... is electronic the new black?
E-textiles promise to revolutionize the textile and apparel industries. Smart clothing will sense and respond appropriately to changes in our body state, such as heart rate, respiration and temperature, as well as to our external environment. Fabric as a microelectronic substrate could enable radical new visions for clothing. A computer screen that drapes like cloth could be powered by photovoltaic fibres. However, for this programmable, electronic wardrobe to be convincing many obstacles need to be overcome.

Truly smart clothing will have to withstand the wear and tear demanded of traditional garments. If a sleeve snags or rips a smart garment must re-route so it still works. The marriage of electronics with a human body that sweats and gets caught in the rain, combined with hostile laundering processes, is not an ideal partnership.

50

50
The German company Infineon Technologies are investigating the possibility of using body heat to power electronic clothing. Heat-coupling elements integrated into fabric can generate electrical energy because of the difference in temperature between the body and surrounding clothes. Thermogenerators could be integrated into clothing, replacing batteries for electronic applications that require only small amounts of power.

51/53
The SCOTTeVEST (SeV) combines traditional clothing, technology and luggage. Up to 42 pockets enable the wearer to carry and connect many portable electronic devices. The addition of a removable PowerFLEX solar panel (by Global Solar) means the user can recharge USB compatible devices on the move.

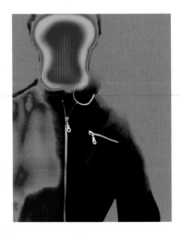

50
Infineon Technologies
Body as battery

51
SCOTTeVEST
X-ray of pocketed gadgets

52/53
SCOTTeVEST
Solar SeV Finetex

53

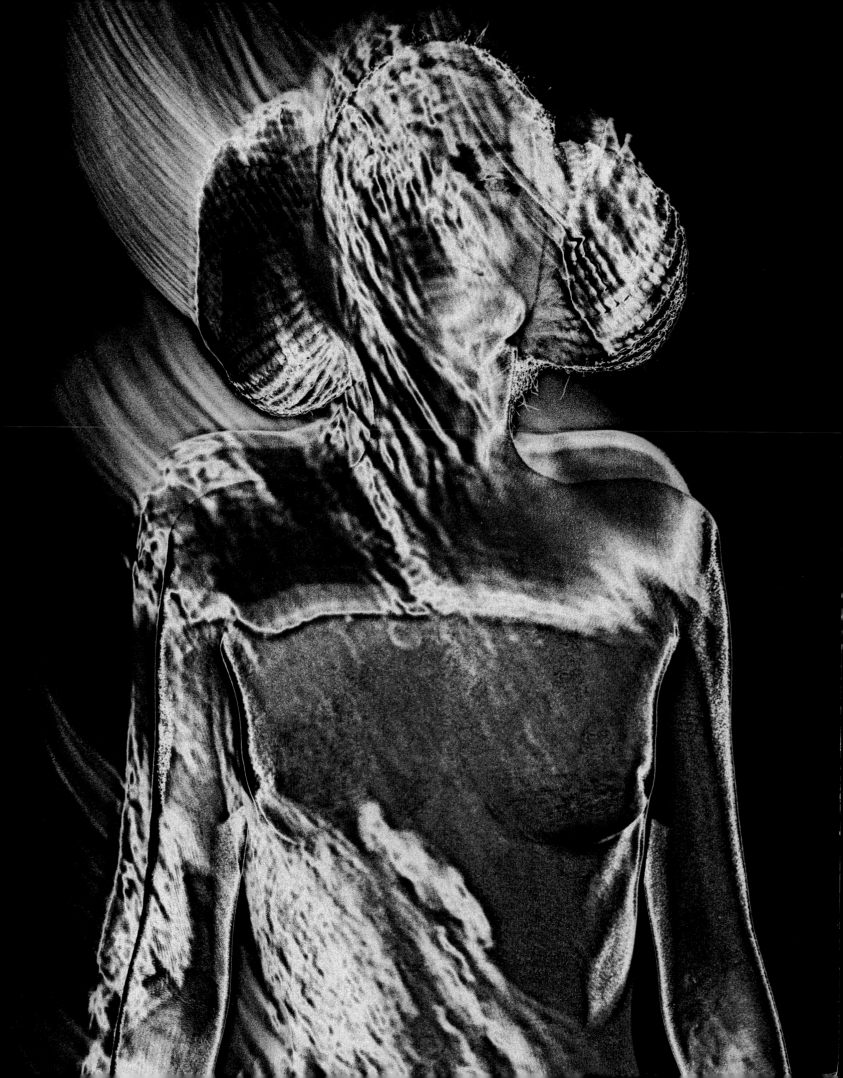

The high development costs of electronics are certainly not compatible with the low margins of fashion and textiles. The consequences of surrounding the body all day everyday with electronics and radio waves are as yet unknown. Contrary to much tech-hype, we are unlikely to be wearing phones in collars or computers on sleeves. Wearability means that instead of placing electronics on textiles, electronics will have to become textiles. These will have to be squashable, washable and, ultimately, desirable. Electronic clothing that offers intelligence with elegance is still many years away.

If people are stressed at the thought of putting together an outfit now, imagine the new worries that might be added by smart clothing. As well as 'Does this shirt match this skirt?', will we ask 'Is this dress functionally compatible with this bag?' If clothing can act as a conduit to a phone, PDA or entry system, what happens in a case of theft? Clothing has always been an expression of identity, but what if our electronic identity is stolen along with our scarf? Will we fear our jackets being hacked? Will Prada provide an emergency cancellation/de-activation service for a lost raincoat? In these instances, the line that currently separates what we understand as fashion and electronic products would begin to dissolve.

54
In his 'High-Tech' collection, Gaultier's black leather coat had computer circuitry embroidered onto panels that were safety-pinned in place punk style. Real microelectronic components such as capacitors became decoration.

55
Chalayan's 'Echoform' collection featured a showpiece Aeroplane Dress. Made of glass fibre and resin, it concealed a battery, gears and wheels that were activated by an internal switch operated by the model on the runway. Like the moveable flaps on the wings of an aircraft, sections of the dress slowly slid open to reveal the flesh beneath. Chalayan explains, 'I saw something very bodily about aircraft, I wanted to literally turn one into a dress that almost looks like parts of a wing. I wanted to create the effect that, even when the body was in repose, it was going through speed – I like the contradiction. In many ways I think technology magnifies the body and its functions.'

56
Fashion designers have appropriated computer circuitry as a decorative pattern to signal a futuristic aesthetic and perhaps to infer a future of electric fashion. In this vein, Alexander McQueen's Autumn/Winter 1999/2000 collection for Givenchy featured android-like models wearing bodysuits printed with luminescent computer circuitry.

54
Jean-Paul Gaultier
Autumn/Winter 1981

55
Hussein Chalayan
Autumn/Winter 1999/2000

56
Alexander McQueen for Givenchy
Autumn/Winter 1999/2000

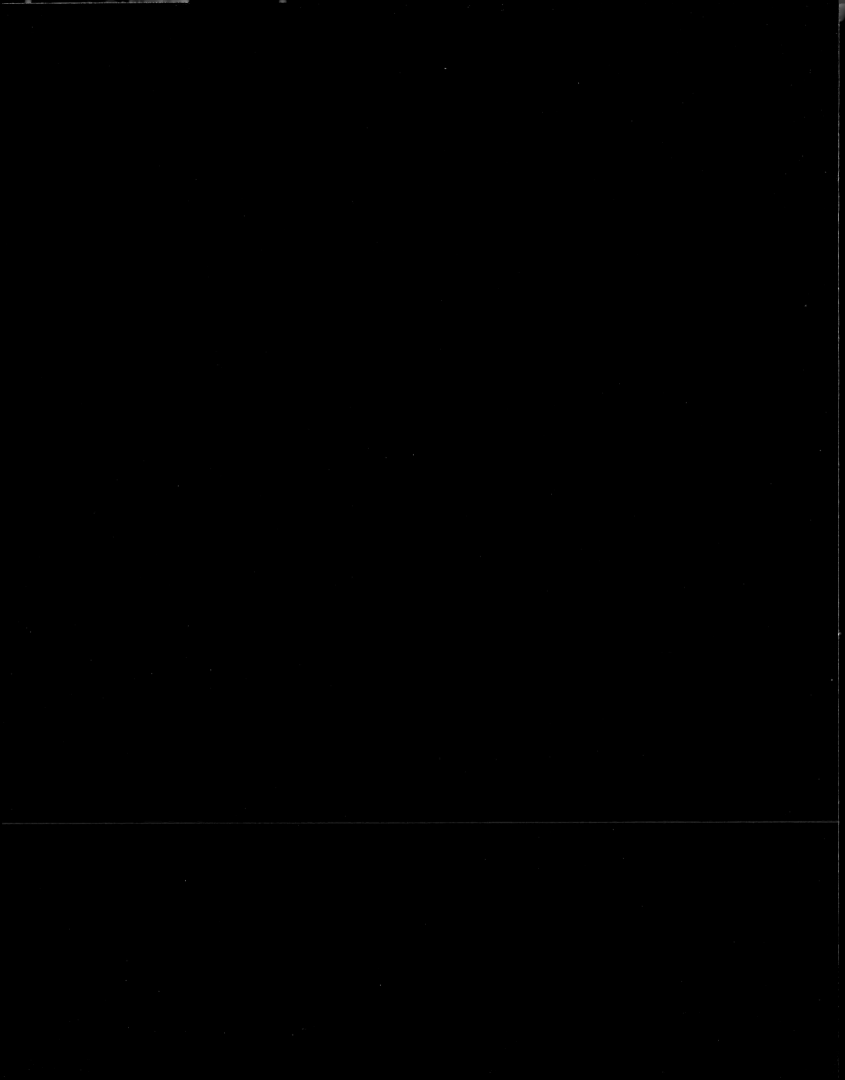

CHAPTER THREE/
THE GROWABLE SUIT

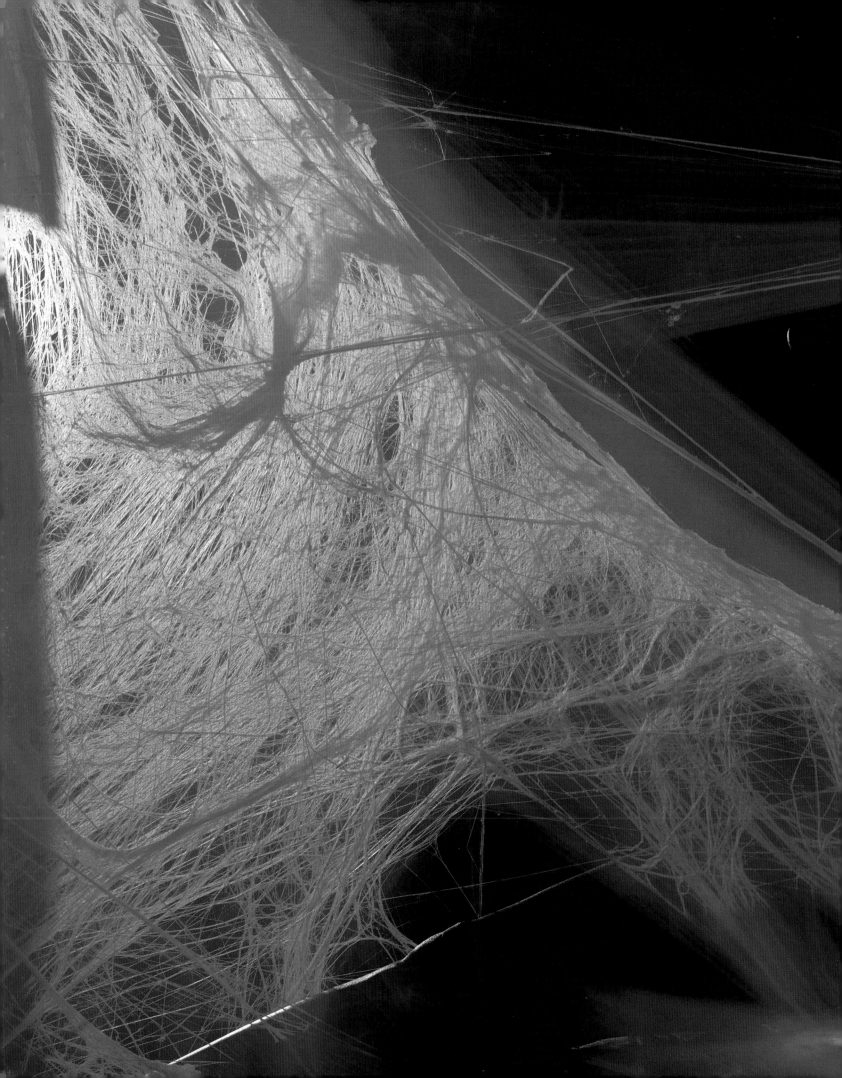

issey
miyake
2001

Once again our society is poised to make dramatic changes based upon developments in science and technology. Will fashion be able to afford to keep the same old methodology?...I believe that technology can function only as long as we have the ability to imagine, a sense of curiosity and a love for our fellow men.

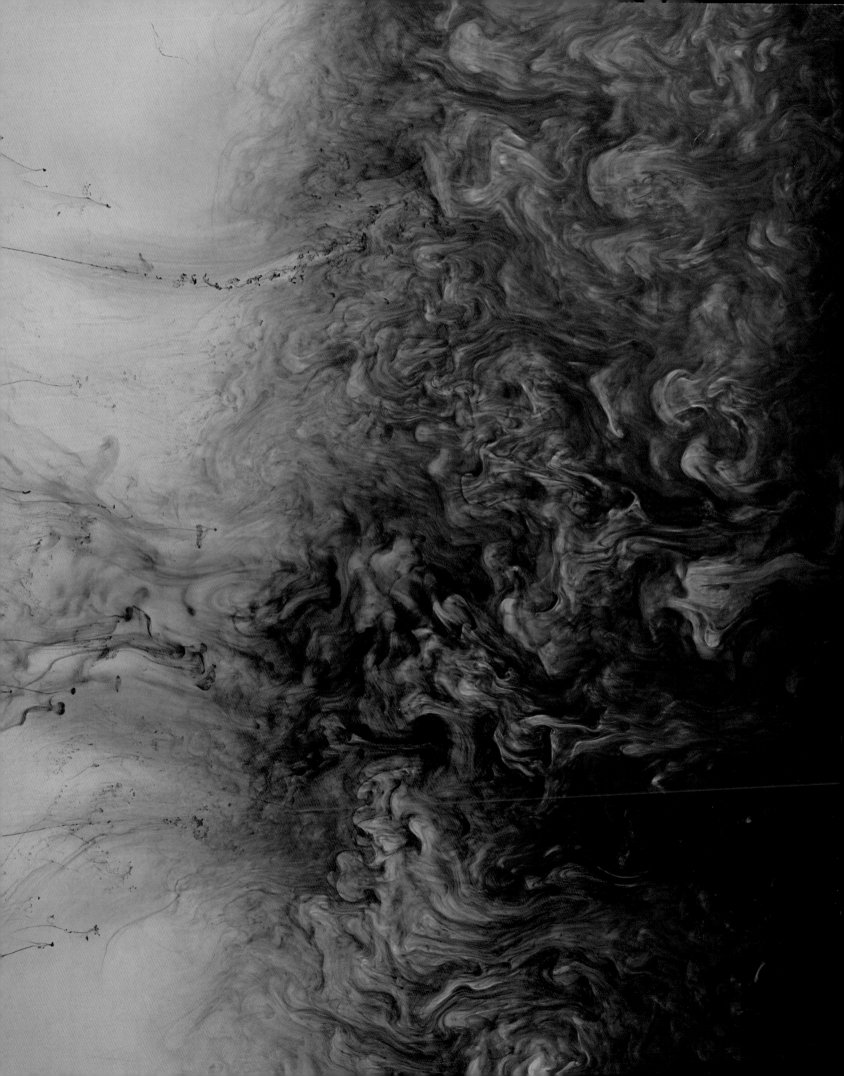

The history of clothing charts man's command of the natural world. Garments created by indigenous cultures can teach us much about textile and clothing technologies. Over millennia, Arctic peoples such as the Inuit have honed their skills to exploit the different qualities of animal skins for warmth, waterproofing and breathability. Gut and fish skin are harnessed to make waterproof coats, parkas and boots; reindeer fur, seal and bird skins, all excellent insulators from the cold, are made into under-garments and outerwear.[1] In the developed world, humans no longer need to rely so directly on animals for survival, but the synthesis of biological systems and materials is of interest to scientists designing the materials of tomorrow. In a burgeoning era of *biotechnology*, we are not only copying nature through *biomimicry* (mimicking biology), and harnessing nature in *bioactive* materials, but also growing our own versions of nature using *tissue engineering*.

In his work with Issey Miyake for A-POC, Dai Fujiwara muses on the future of cloth innovation, wondering what fabric will be:

Perhaps a hybrid from a silkworm and a spider, or polyester extracted from a rice plant? The concept of 'nature' and what is natural may inevitably change.[2]

...spider-silk

Humans have been spinning silk from silkworms since at least 3000 BC, but the ability to produce spider silk has always evaded scientists. Dragline silk, used to make the web, has unique material qualities – pound for pound it is stronger than steel cable yet twice as elastic as nylon and ultra-light. These extreme performance characteristics make it highly desirable for many applications and, with the help of biotechnology, commercial production is coming closer.

57

The Inuit people often use the skins of auks or little auks to make parkas. The feather-side of the skin is turned to the inside and worn against the body as an inner garment, usually under an outer parka of sealskin. Birdskin clothes are light, warm and waterproof, but they tear easily. The English word anorak comes from *anoraq*, meaning 'a piece of clothing' in the language of the Inuit. Like other forms of Inuit technology, Inuit clothing fascinates by its apparently simple design and great effectiveness. The parka pictured here was made by the Inuit of the Smith Sound area in northern Greenland. It was collected by the American explorer Robert Peary sometime between 1891 and 1909 on one of his Arctic expeditions.

58

Women examining the wondrous invention of 'manmade' silk at a fashion show in London. An early example of scientific research synthesizing nature and one that was to revolutionize fashion.

57
Birdskin parka, late 19th century

58
Synthetic silk, 1926

Garments made from a spider-silk cloth could mean breathable, gossamer-thin fabrics that are tough, light, don't tear, and stretch for comfort – perfect material for surgical implants, protective clothing, leisure and sportswear. Eveningwear created with this fibre might look dangerously delicate but the slinkiest dress could actually be supremely robust.

Biotechnology researchers are investigating various techniques for the manufacture of a fibre with the properties of spider silk. The first task is to generate the silk-producing protein itself, the second is to emulate the spider's complex spinning process. Spiders are cannibalistic and therefore unsuited to farming. Instead, scientists are using *transgenics*, a process where the crucial gene from the spider is transferred to genetic matter in other living organisms to mass-produce the spider-silk protein. Experimental harvesting has been achieved in bacteria, plants and even in animals – E.coli, tobacco and goats can all be genetically engineered to produce the dragline-silk protein.[3]

Spinning the protein into a viable fibre has proved rather more difficult. At Spinox, a company founded on research conducted by Professor Fritz Vollrath and Dr David Knight at Oxford University, scientists are developing a biomimetic system that copies how the spider spins silk. Engineering biosilk is a desirable goal since the silk would be recyclable and the process would be a sustainable, non-polluting alternative to petrochemical-based fibres. According to Dr Knight:

Spinox is an excellent example of how we can use nature's ingenuity to help us develop new processes and materials with quite exceptional properties in an eco-friendly way.[4]

59

In a series of experiments during the 1950s scientists injected laboratory spiders with psychotropic drugs to study the effect on their ability to spin silk. The resulting webs showed highly irregular patterns.

60

The thread of the cross orb spider *Araneus diadematus* is very elastic and can be stretched 30–40 per cent before it breaks. Steel can be stretched only 8 per cent and nylon around 20 per cent. Polynesian fishermen use the thread of the golden orb web spider *Nephila* as fishing line. During the Second World War the threads of *Araneus diadematus*, *Zilla atrica*, *Argiope aurantia* and other orb weavers were used as hairs in measuring equipment. The Americans used the threads of the black widow spider *Latrodectus* in their telescopic gun sights.

61

In a programme called BioSteel, Nexia Biotechnologies in Montreal have genetically engineered (transgenic) goats to secrete spider silk proteins in their milk. Once isolated, these proteins can be spun into silk. This is a costly and technically difficult process, and the company has chosen to focus on spinning BioSteel proteins into nanometer diameter fibres for medical and microelectronic applications. A commercially viable method of spinning spider silk to produce a yarn or fibre for fashion remains a dream.

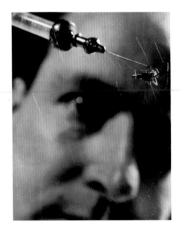

59
Experiment with spider web, 1955

60
Spider web

61
Nexia Biotechnologies
Transgenic goats

With many companies and research departments competing to be the first to have a commercial spider-silk fibre, we can expect this to emerge in the near future.

…living clothes

'Clothing is an obvious habitat for biological micro-machines.'[5] This is the belief of a team of researchers, led by Dr Alex Fowler at the University of Massachusetts, Dartmouth, who are creating bioactive fabrics containing living bacteria. These fabrics could be made into clothing that is self-cleaning, odour-eating, waterproof and healing. Genetically engineered bacteria are inserted into hollow fibres to cultivate colonies of micro-organisms that can live and breed off proteins contained in sweat and stains. An odour-eating garment would need just to be worn regularly so that it could function – valuable for running shoes or sportswear. Wearers would be oblivious to the harmless bacteria working away on their behalf. Other applications might be drug-producing bandages where a healing antiseptic can be delivered instantly to the skin, or protective clothing that incorporates cellular sensors to detect bioterror agents in the air. Living fabric is still in its early stages, but Fowler's team suggests cellular micro-machines will create the functional clothing of the future.

…growable couture

As discussed above, bacteria can be harnessed to add functionality to fabrics, but they might also be used to grow fabric or clothing itself. Dr David Hepworth, a biologist and materials scientist at the British-based firm Cellucomp, proposes fabricating clothing from cellulose using bacterial cultures.

Cellulose is the most abundant renewable resource on the planet. It is the main component of wood, cotton and paper. Traditional production of natural fibres like

62
A colour lithograph caricature of female dress and accessories constructed from fish and crustaceans. Wearing shellfish is no longer a matter for ridicule – Chitosan, a natural substance taken from the shells of crabs, shrimps and krill, is now exploited for its antibacterial, healing effect in bandages, fibres and fabrics. A blend of Chitosan and polyester, labelled Chitopoly, is used for clothing, such as babywear and underwear, for those with sensitive skin.

63
Shark skin viewed under an electron microscope reveals 'dermal denticles' that help to reduce drag and streamline the shark in water. Shark skin is very rough and historically was used as sandpaper.

64/65
Researchers at Speedo studied shark denticles when creating their biomimetic Fastskin fabric, which increases a swimmer's speed by reducing drag. Male and female specific and even stroke specific bodysuits feature different fabrics for the various parts of the body.

62
G. Spratt
Fish dress cartoon, 1830

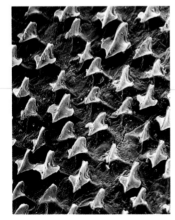

63
Shark skin

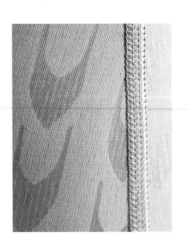

64
Speedo Fastskin II fabric, 2004

65
Speedo Fastskin II bodysuits, 2004

cotton can be wasteful and energy inefficient since the plant has to be broken down to extract the cellulose fibre and the remainder discarded. According to Dr Hepworth, our reliance on natural materials has come full circle. We started out wearing animal skins and cutting wood but became divorced from nature as we gravitated towards making things from oil-based materials. He believes bioengineered materials will offer a sustainable alternative:

What I find interesting is how far people are prepared to go in terms of making use of living organisms. You don't need to destroy nature, or break it down using chemicals to extract the bit you need...Cellulose grown from scratch would be biodegradable and much more like farming than an industrial process. Nature can grow things for us to make exactly what we want with no waste.[6]

Clothes would be grown in a *bioreactor* under conditions favourable to rapid growth, encouraging the bacteria to multiply and produce cellulose. Hepworth calculates that it should be possible to grow clothes within hours. Once a garment is completed, the bacteria could remain dormant ready to be revitalized as the wearer wishes by introducing fresh nutrient. For example, spraying a glucose solution along the hem might cause a garment to lengthen overnight, or rips and tears could self-repair with one quick application.

Cellular couture would be biodegradable and readily recyclable. Disposable protective or medical clothing, childrenswear and sportswear might all benefit. And what better parallel for fashion, which by its very nature is about constant re-invention? In future we might compost our wardrobes and grow something new, or, at the very least, return it to the store for recycling.

66
Britsh artists Heather Ackroyd and Dan Harvey work with the natural process of photosynthesis to create patterned effects or images on living surfaces. The tiger-striped effect on this coat was achieved by denying light to certain areas of growing grass so that they became a yellow colour. A living, biodegradable garment provides a transient fashion statement and an alternative to real animal fur.

67
LifeGem is an American company that creates memorial diamonds from the carbon in the ashes of deceased loved ones. By heating the carbon to high temperatures it is converted to graphite, which is then cut to the desired style. The human body can now be worn as a piece of decorative jewelry.

66
Heather Ackroyd and Dan Harvey
Tiger-striped grass coat, 1991

67
LifeGem
Round cut diamond, 2004

At present, biomaterials created by tissue engineering are more familiar to the medical world where skin and even more complex organs can be grown in a laboratory for implant into the human body. In London, Tobie Kerridge and Nikki Stott, research associates at the Royal College of Art, are collaborating with scientists Professor Larry Hench and Dr Ian Thompson at Imperial College's Tissue Engineering and Regenerative Medicine Centre to create 'biojewelry'. In a pioneering project uniting biotechnology and design, they propose to manufacture rings from biological material donated by a couple who wish to make a symbolic commitment to one another by exchanging this biojewelry. The completed rings will be fabricated from grown bone mass and subsequently treated like any other material, possibly finished in a traditional manner with a precious metal such as silver or gold. The end result could be as stunning as any piece produced in the normal way but with added emotional value.

The couple undergo an operation to extract cells from their jawbones that can be grown to provide the raw material for the jewelry. Cells are implanted into a foam scaffold that is suspended in a bioactive solution inside a chamber. This unit is constantly rotated through 360 degrees to counteract gravity, ensuring the bone grows evenly. The designers wish to predetermine the shape of the bone at this stage, and once it is grown it will be milled and treated like a normal material. Kerridge notes:

Strangely enough the tools they have in the medical laboratory are not so different from the machinery that is used in our jewelry-making studio, cutting implements, lathes, etc.[7]

68

Tobie Kerridge and Nikki Stott, researchers at the Royal College of Art, London, have been working with tissue engineering scientists at Imperial College on a project to create 'biojewelry' formed from human bone. A patient undergoes a minor operation to extract a sample of bone tissue from the jaw. This sample can then be processed and used to grow a bone culture in the laboratory.

69

This image of concentric circles shows the growth of bone crystal in the laboratory.

70

On the left a porous, bioactive ceramic scaffold is used to grow the bone tissue. On the right, a prototype model of a ring demonstrates how biojewelry might look. Here, cow marrowbone was substituted for human bone and combined with etched silver. Kerridge and Stott have been interviewing couples who are happy to act as guinea pigs and undergo operations to provide the team with bone cells to grow their jewelry. The final rings will be exchanged in a ceremony that sees two people giving literally a piece of themselves to a cherished partner.

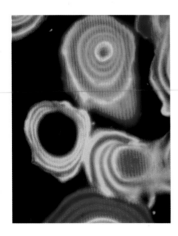

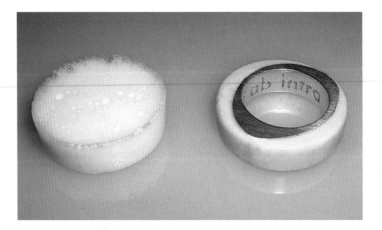

68
Biopsy to extract bone cells

69
Bone cell division

70
Foam scaffold and bone-ring prototype, 2004

Aesthetic decisions will be taken in conjunction with the donating couple for the final design and finishing. Kerridge explains that the real value and symbolism in the objects that these people will wear is that the material comes from each other. They will literally be giving a piece of themselves. The team is keen to explore the moral issues raised during this process and the discussion of ethics, ownership and legality will be central to the project's development. The researchers believe this project is about taking biotechnology and giving it a context to which people can relate. Human and animal bones have been used for jewelry by diverse cultures and civilizations to symbolize death and departed spirits, but here the bone is of the living, grown to symbolize life. Although commercialization is not the intention of this particular project, Kerridge anticipates a market for biotech designs:

In the future it might be a shop, or a service that is negotiated between a surgeon and a jeweller, [and] the first place the consumer might go would be the jeweller.[8]

Biotechnology designer services may proliferate with 'body salons' offering quick surgical or DNA extractions to harvest biomaterial for all manner of uses. Human skin can now be grown in a laboratory environment quite easily – it is theoretically possible to grow your own skin to make a leather jacket from yourself for yourself. Today I'm wearing me.

...second skins

This may seem reminiscent of Frankenstein, but it is a reality being explored by the Tissue Culture & Art Project (TC&A), established in Perth, Australia in 1996. Bio-artists Oron Catts and Ionat Zurr are interested in creating semi-living objects such as Victimless Leather, a miniature garment grown from animal cells. However, the project

71

Inspired by the French artist Orlan, who transforms her appearance by using plastic surgery as an artistic technique, the Belgian designer Van Beirendonck and the make-up artist Geoff Portass created a futuristic make-up with 3D protuberances on models' faces. As Van Beirendonck explained: 'All the metamorphoses of faces were first worked out on the computer. Then we made the latex implants in such a way that on the day of the show all we had to do was stick them on the models and cover them with foundation for the effect to be as natural as possible.'

72

The Fibre Reactive dress is made from silk with *Pycnoporus coccineus* (a fungi commonly known as orange bracket) growing out of it. As artist-in-residence at SymbioticA (The Art and Science Collaborative Research Laboratory at the University of Western Australia), Donna Franklin explored the use of fungi on fibres and fabric; here they form layers of vivid orange petals .

73

Based at SymbioticA, bio-artists Oron Catts and Ionat Zurr work at the junction of biotechnology and art. Their Victimless Leather miniature coat is grown from cultured cells. The artists' intentions are to 'confront people with the moral implications of wearing parts of dead animals for protective and aesthetic reasons' and to 'raise the possibility of wearing "leather" without killing an animal.'

71
Walter Van Beirendonck
Autumn/Winter 1998/9

72
Donna Franklin
Fibre Reactive dress, 2004

73
Tissue Culture & Art Project
Victimless Leather, 2004

74
KnoWear
Skinthetic: Chanel, 2001

is concerned with tissue engineering as a medium for artistic expression, not as a commercial product, and wishes to promote an ethical debate on the use of biotechnology in art and design. TC&A outlines its manifesto as follows:

These are parts of complex organisms which are sustained alive outside of the body and coerced to grow in predetermined shapes. These evocative objects are a tangible example that brings into question deep-rooted perceptions of life and identity, concept of self, and the position of the human in regard to other living beings and the environment. We are interested in the new discourses and new ethics/epistemologies that surround issues of partial life and the contestable future scenarios they are offering us.[9]

...fashion as implant

TC&A is part of an emerging community of designers and artists who are engaging with the creative possibilities and ethical concerns posed by biotechnology. Inevitably, designers are drawn to the issue of the commercial exploitation of biotechnology for consumer products. One future use may be biomaterials engineered as fashion implants, especially for branding and advertising. This vision of a world where the body and brand merge has been taken up by Peter Allen and Carla Murray of KnoWear, a design practice based in Cataumet, Massachusetts, in their conceptual project Skinthetic:

Where in 2000 we as consumers put labels on our bodies through the act of clothing, by 2020 we will be implanting designed body parts that are not only genetically coded but also will bear the signs and identities of the couture and product house that have created them.[10]

74/76
KnoWear's Skinthetic project explores the effects of branding and mass media on a person's identity. As implant and explant technology becomes more sophisticated, and branding more entwined with commodity culture, labels and bodies could become one. Here, the signature Chanel quilting is applied seamlessly both to the garment's surface and to the body's, in the form of a three-dimensional tattoo.

75
KnoWear
Skinthetic branded implant

76
KnoWear
Skinthetic runway simulation

In Skinthetic, the consumer doesn't wear a fashion brand or logo; they become it. Taking Chanel as a case study, and using digital designs, Allen and Murray show how the famous quilting from the iconic leather-and-chain handbag would look when it became a pattern on the naked flesh of fashion models. The resulting image is of an instantly recognizable but disturbing designer implant.

The projects described in this chapter anticipate a coming era of biotechnology that will permeate all our lives. However, given the power to change nature and to design life, how far should designers go? The ethical, ecological and economic arguments surrounding biotechnology are complex, and although its use in medicine has gained a measure of public acceptance because of its obvious benefits, manipulating nature for consumer products is likely to meet with more resistance. Will today's lifesaving medical technology be used to design tomorrow's fashions?

Tobie Kerridge and his partners received a positive response to their biojewelry project, suggesting a favourable market exists. Bioengineered materials can offer not only creative possibilities but also alternatives to rare materials or polluting processes. Nonetheless, there is potential for abuse or causing offence. Fashion has always courted controversy, and is not known for its ethical concerns. Will we covet cellulose stilettos or fantasize about 'fur' coats cultured from human hair? What shocks us today we enthusiastically embrace tomorrow. For now, we can only muse on when and how fashion and biotechnology shall meet.

77
In Van Beirendonck's 1997 book *Mutilate*, he is transformed into a scaly reptile – a transgenic Walter. The designer admits to being fascinated by cloning and the manipulation of the body: 'In my "Fetish for Beauty" presentation, a big part of the show was "talking" about how, in the future, plastic surgery will be used to do personal "body-statements" instead of trying to create the perfect beauty (as prescribed by the environment/community/beauty-norms). I foresee perfectly that plastic surgery will be used in the future in a creative, adventurous way. Not only to recreate a special bodyshape, but also to improve our way of performing, working and loving.'

78/79
Microbiologist Dr A.W.S.M. van Egeraat collaborated with the Belgian fashion designer Martin Margiela on his project 9/4/1615. They used bacteria and fungi to create a look of decay on the garments shown in a retrospective exhibition of Margiela's work.

80
Jeweller Shaun Leane's body sculpture for Alexander McQueen used a human skeleton to create a mould – might future high-fashion pieces be grown from human bone cells?

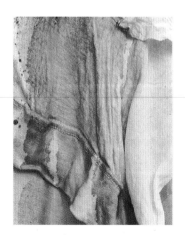

77
Walter Van Beirendonck
Mutilate, 1997

78
Martin Margiela
Red bacteria on cotton, 1997

79
Martin Margiela
Pink yeast on cotton, 1997

80
Shaun Leane for Alexander McQueen
Spring/Summer 1998

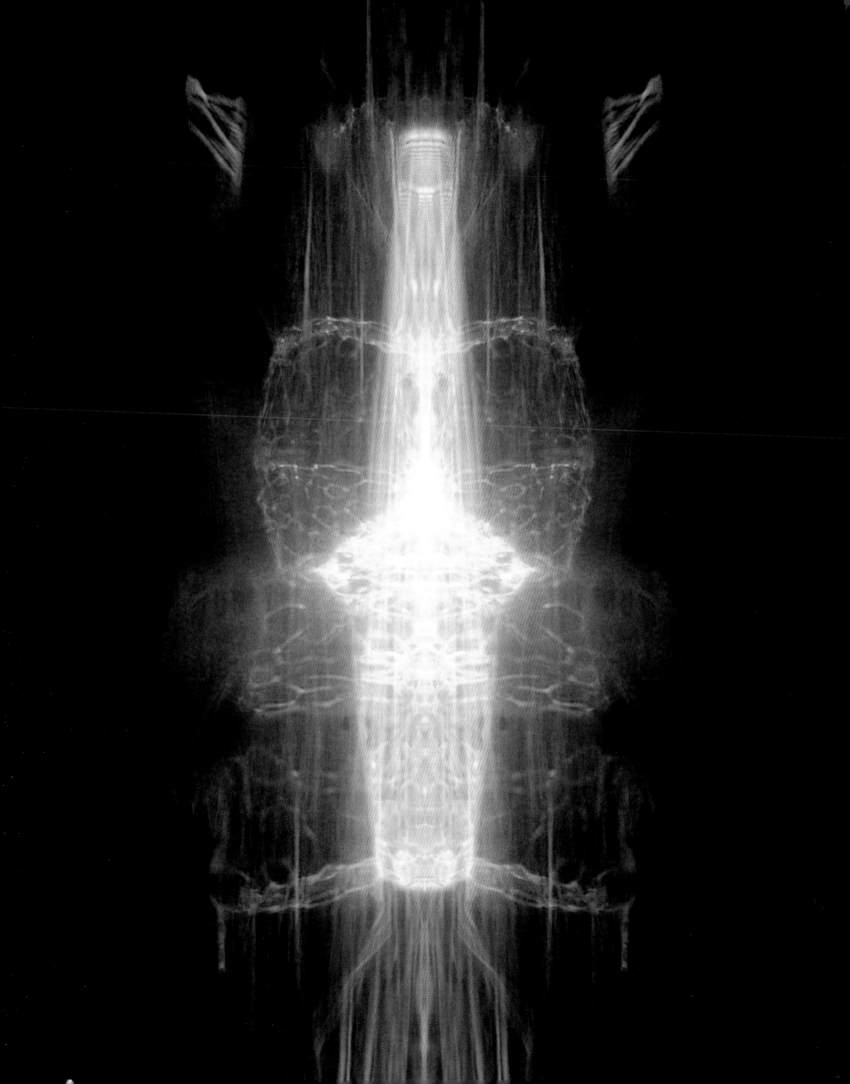

CHAPTER FOUR/ THE INVISIBLE COAT

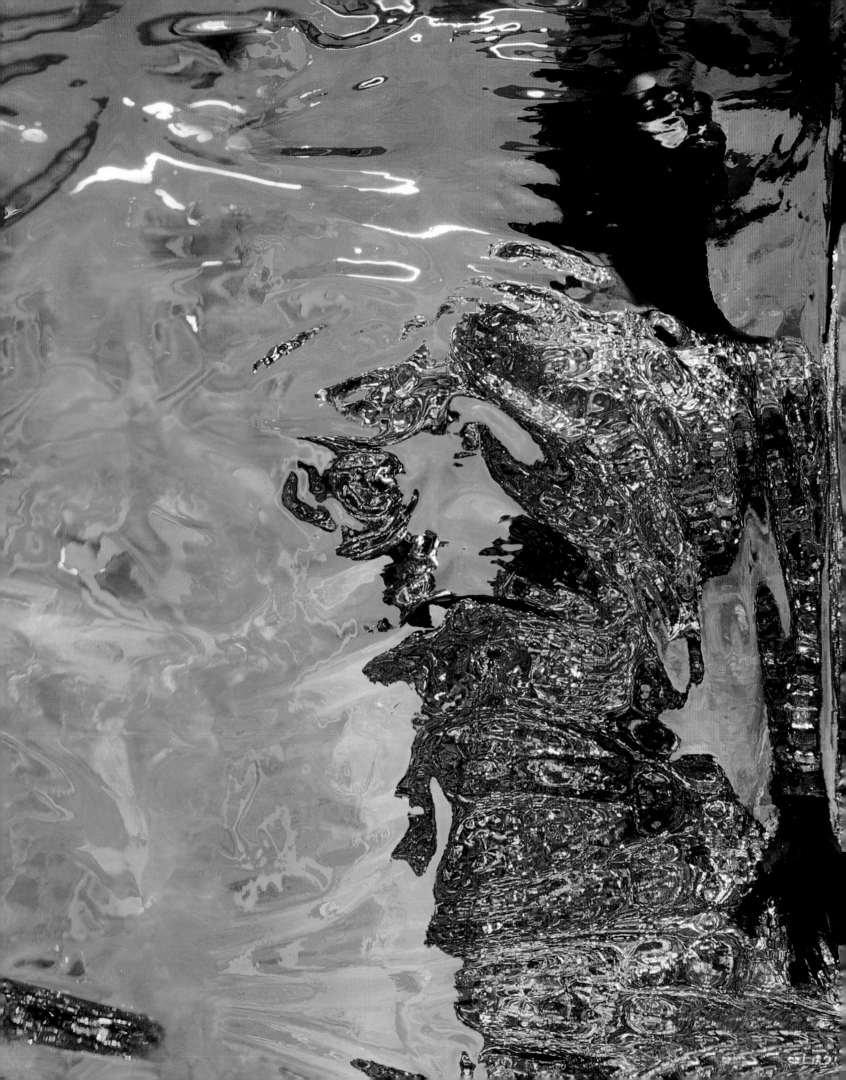

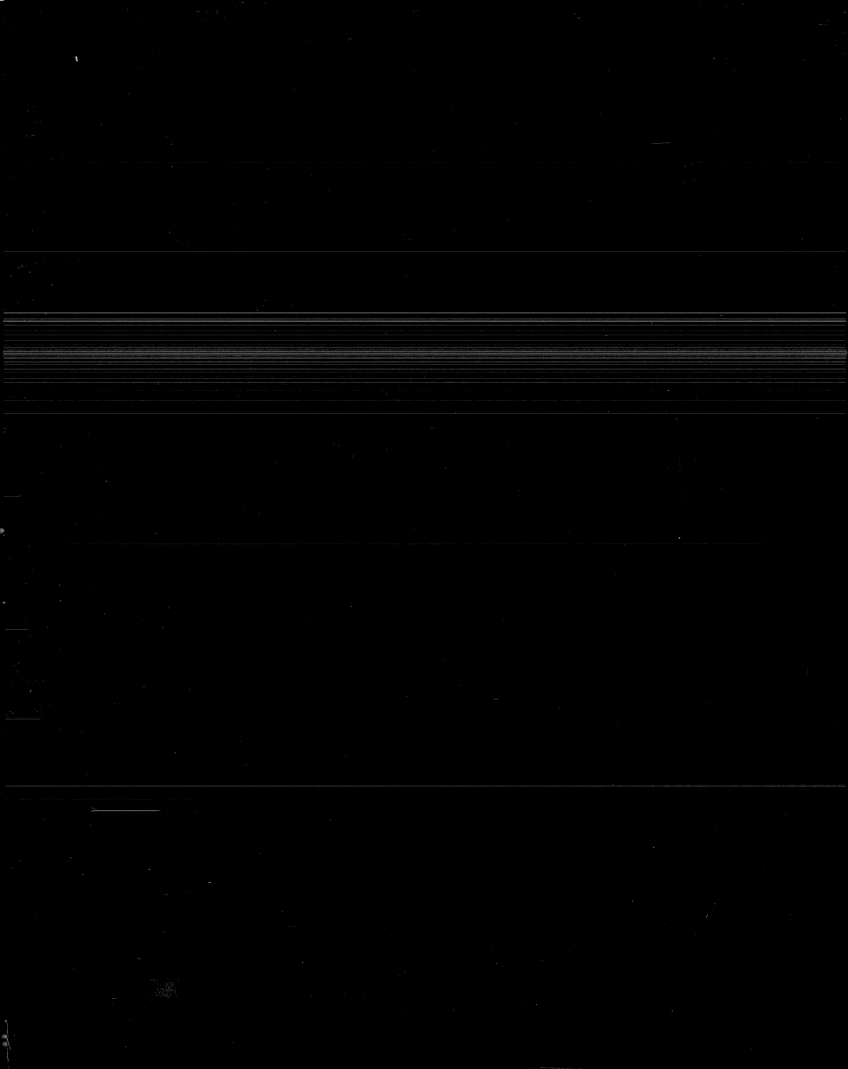

walter
van
beirendonck
2004

It would be fantastic if Haute Couture could again become a laboratory for fashion. That would make it relevant once more. I really do like the research and statements that Cardin made back in the 1960s, he was my first hero. Fashion, science, technology, craftsmanship and fantasy should work hand in hand. I am a volunteer if a big couture house is willing to invest in such an adventure…Cardin, Courrèges…?

81
Victor & Rolf
Autumn/Winter 2002

Victor & Rolf's Autumn/Winter 2002 ready-to-wear collection created the illusion of something that research laboratories the world over are working on for real – a fabric variously described as *chameleon camouflage*, digital cloth or a textile display. As the models passed the audience, the fabric of the clothes streamed with film footage of traffic in the street and clouds racing across the sky. Brilliant blue detailing in the outfits was replaced by digitally projected images, a process known as bluescreening. Simultaneously, each model was projected onto giant screens on either side of the runway, placing the girl in a filmic background against which she appeared camouflaged, even invisible. Bluescreening is a special effect more commonly used in film and television, but in the hands of Victor Horsting and Rolf Snoeren it became the inspiration for a fashion collection.

81/84
Also known as chroma-keying, bluescreening is a process used in movie-making and television where anything painted in a brilliant blue pigment can be digitally isolated and replaced with another image. In the images below, blue areas within the clothing are substituted by a mountain range, sky or city scapes – the body disappearing into a virtual background. Estimates as to when this might become a fabric reality vary wildly between five and fifty years.

...:wearable media

Dress is a complex form of non-verbal communication. It can make the wearer stand out but can also serve to conceal, enabling the person to 'fit in'. Traditionally, we change clothes so we look appropriate for each new situation. In nature, too, changeable states are desirable for various reasons: to mask and protect, to attract a mate or to signal status. Clothing already performs these functions both implicitly and explicitly. The advent of a programmable fabric display would increase these established roles for dress, resulting in a kind of hyper-clothing. If the boundaries blur between dress and media, will fashion designers become 'content providers' and will fashion become part of the entertainment and media industries? Will advertisers regard 'wearable media' as the most direct form of product promotion and target 'body space' on our clothing?[1] Currently, consumers are willing to pay for the privilege of wearing merchandise with a company's logo. Are we about to see an era of brands paying the consumer?

82
Victor & Rolf
Autumn/Winter 2002

83
Victor & Rolf
Autumn/Winter 2002

84
Victor & Rolf
Autumn/Winter 2002

Lunar Design Inc. of Los Angeles investigated wearable media in 2001 for their BLU project. It was a conceptual exploration of how clothing, *flexible displays* and *wireless networking* technologies might come together. Based on digital displays becoming as thin, cheap and flexible as paper, three scenarios were designed: Carta, Your Ad Here, and Dada. Carta imagines a cycle-courier wearing a kind of active A–Z jacket. Its surface displays the cyclist's route and progress using *Bluetooth* and *GPS* technologies. Lunar comments: 'the glowing path of your trek becomes an artful reminder of where you've been and where you're going.'[2] Your Ad Here, a second scenario using the same technology, describes a display garment as being a 'high-tech sandwich board'. Tad Toulis, the BLU project leader, proposes you could fund the latest 'wearable upgrades' in technology by renting out space on your jacket:

Displays composed of a matrix of microscopic beads pick up radio frequencies that orient the array into recognizable patterns. Since it can now change colour and image, the garment itself becomes a street-level billboard. Garments made of this material could take established notions of label and brand to entirely new dimensions.[3]

Lunar's third scenario, Dada, suggests a subscription service. Fashion brands might offer downloads of the latest colours, prints and graphics. For instance, $200 a month could buy a 'couture' service from Chanel or $20 a month would obtain the chain-store option from Gap. The identity consumers currently associate with a particular brand, such as exclusive checks (Burberry) or a logo (Nike's 'swoosh'), would be rendered digitally; fashion as pure information. Indeed, Lunar believes that a combination of performance art and social commentary could open the door to a new vein of modern fashion.

85/86
In Lunar Design's conceptual BLU project, garments become active digital displays capable of presenting information on the move – updating an A–Z jacket with location and traffic data or selling advertising space. Using wireless networking, a garment might receive and display any information the wearer chooses, downloading live from the Internet. With a rapid refresh rate, moving images such as personal movie clips, television or other moving media could be streamed to those around you. The future digital display garment could be a gallery, billboard, diary or personal assistant.

87
The first generation of clothes capable of displaying digital information will probably consist of small flexible OLED (organic light-emitting diode) screens sewn into conventional garments and powered by batteries.

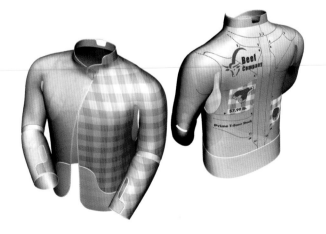

85
Lunar
BLU – Carta, 2001

86
Lunar
BLU – Your Ad Here, 2001

87
Pioneer
Colour OLED displays in a coat, 2002

A computer screen that is fluid like silk and has a surface flowing with crystal-clear moving images is an idea that, unusually, has appeal for both the fashion and technology industries. In its simplest form, this cloth could act like a computer screen, a blank canvas onto which the wearer would download patterns or information. You might opt to wear an iconic Warhol 'Marilyn' print one minute and a Pucci design the next – or both at the same time. In a more dynamic mode, it may give life to a fabric design – a paisley pattern might swirl around changing colour and scale. A textile display might respond to body sensors that monitor data such as heart rate or skin temperature, it might react to motion or to the wearer's location or social situation. It could be dynamically changing and programmable on the move. Hence, in full interactive mode, a striped fabric might blur if it was caught suddenly by a breeze or the wearer started to run, and a polka-dot motif might 'wash away' with rain. Alternatively, the wearer might choose to relay a favourite band playing, to advertise the latest blockbuster movie or a news channel: 'Today, I'm wearing CNN.'

The dream of a fabric display is much hyped in technology circles, having been promised for the last decade, but is still not much closer to realization, and remains the Holy Grail of textiles. Some researchers, however, advocate a more down-to-earth approach. Maggie Orth, who, with Joanna Berzowska, founded International Fashion Machines Inc. (IFM) in Cambridge, Massachusetts in 2001, has observed that:

When you talk to people who are trying to develop displays on textiles, so many of them are trying to create something that is so far off, they want video-quality imagery on cloth right now!...The primary issue is not technology, it's about how it communicates and what it can do visually.[4]

88
A model wearing a newspaper-print dress is camouflaged against a newstand. Print media was used to decorative effect in fashion for much of the twentieth century. News clippings turned into fabric prints were a signature of the surrealist fashion designer Elsa Schiaparelli in the 1930s.

89
British designer Katherine Hamnett has famously used T-shirts as fashion/protest 'billboards'. When she met Prime Minister Mrs Thatcher at a reception for designers at 10 Downing Street during British Fashion Week in 1984, Hamnett wore a T-shirt protesting about the UK government's plan to purchase nuclear missiles.

90
A Jens Laugesen design from the SHOWstudio website project of downloadable 'print-your-own' designer T-shirts. A white T-shirt is treated as a blank canvas on which to print a styled image of another garment. The SHOWstudio project indicated how in the future designers might supply their creations in the form of digital files online that could be downloaded and applied by the wearer where and when they wish.

83

88
Newspaper-print dress, 1974

89
Katherine Hamnett
T-shirt politics, 1984

90
Jens Laugesen
Ground Zero, 2002

Orth trained as an artist before embarking on an extended period of study at MIT. While other researchers were developing software applications, Orth was keen to counteract the remoteness of technology, preferring to investigate things people could touch, objects that might communicate, and the relationships that might emerge from this new artistic medium of expression. This led to IFM developing Electric Plaid or E-Plaid.

E-Plaid consists of natural fibres interwoven with conductive stainless-steel yarns and printed with *thermochromic* inks. When an electric current is applied to the material, the conductive fibres heat up, causing the thermochromic inks to change colour. It is an electronically controllable, hand-woven display with simple but changeable colour and pattern. From the beginning it was clothing that inspired Orth:

I found a sample from a wedding dress that was metallic silk organza. It was a decorative Indian fabric that's been made for thousands of years and I looked at it and thought 'that metal thread will conduct electricity' and for me *electro-textiles* just took off from there.[5]

Although E-Plaid, in its present form, is not suitable for clothing because its yarns become heated, it is already finding its way into galleries as interactive textile art. Orth is interested in the expressive and aesthetic possibilities of technology at a personal level, and is looking for answers to questions such as 'Can we make things expressive in a way that they haven't been before?'

...optical camouflage

In addition to being decorative or broadcasting information, a dynamic fabric might reflect its surroundings. If a garment mirrored its environment it would render its wearer

91

The computer display industry is driving research into screens that are thin and flexible enough to roll, fold or put in your pocket.

92

International Fashion Machines' Electric Plaid combines woven electronic circuits, colour-change inks and drive electronics to give a sense of movement to textile designs. Patterns change colour slowly over time to alter the decor of the room. Electric Plaid is a reflective (it does not light up) colour-change medium and when combined with embroidered touch sensors can create interactive textiles and artworks.

93

Organic light-emitting diodes (OLEDs) and polymer light-emitting diodes (PLEDs) are glowing plastic molecules that can be printed onto flexible thin films to make a colour display that is brighter than a liquid crystal display (LCD). OLEDs and PLEDs emit their own light and so are lighter and cheaper than LCDs, which need a light source that requires power and space. In the next few years phones, laptops, PC monitors and even TVs could be using OLED technology – the challenge in such 'always on' applications is durability and at present OLEDs have a short lifespan. OLED and PLED technology may well be used in display clothing of the future and, although some way off, ultimately might be printed directly onto cloth itself.

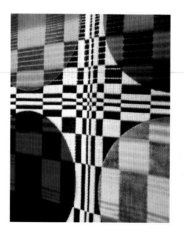

91
E-ink
Flexible microelectronics

92
International Fashion Machines
Electric Plaid

93
OLED display

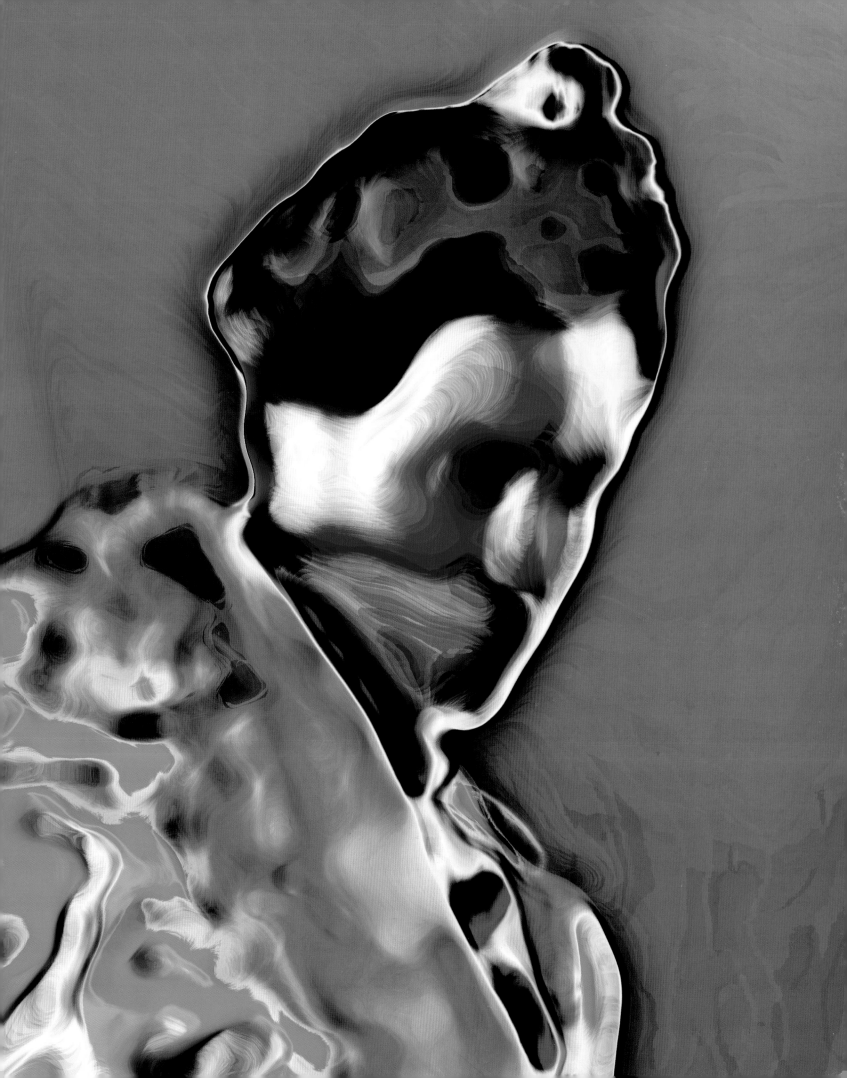

invisible. Discussions of such a material, generally termed chameleon camouflage, frequently reference John McTiernan's 1987 Hollywood movie *Predator*.[6] The figure of the Predator, an alien creature in the jungle, demonstrates the tactical advantage of being invisible to Arnold Schwarzenegger's character and his crew of mercenaries. When still, the Predator is concealed by reflecting the surrounding environment. Only when it stealthily travels through the undergrowth does the figure create a visible blur.

Camouflage mechanisms observed in nature inform much of the contemporary research being conducted in this area. The Blue Morpho butterfly, for example, uses its colourful iridescence not only for courtship but also as camouflage – as it rapidly flaps its wings it virtually disappears against its environment. Its apparently brilliant blue colour is due to the light refraction and reflection performed by its highly complex crystalline surface structure.[7] In a similar way, fish that live near the surface of water use mirror-like scales to reflect light and blend into the dazzling effect of the water's surface, preventing potential predators from seeing any prey from above. The reflective quality of fish scales has not gone unnoticed by the fashion industry – they were used as an early form of sequins in European needlework.[8] Similarly, hummingbirds were used by the Inca in their dress, tying the feathers to cloth at precise angles to obtain optimum iridescence.

From Turkey to China and from India to Mexico, many cultures around the globe have for millennia incorporated mirrors and sequins into dress. However, where ancient civilizations applied mirrors to clothing for protection against evil spirits, twenty-first-century *materials scientists* are engineering microscopic mirrored fabrics to protect soldiers from the enemy. Not surprisingly, the concept of invisible clothing has huge appeal to the military, which is the principal driver of chameleon camouflage research and development.

94
Although it appears to be a shimmering blue, the Blue Morpho butterfly is in fact a sludgy grey-brown. Blue pigments in the natural world are quite rare; most blues are the result of structural design not dye. The design of the wing's surface enables light to be refracted and reflected, filtering out all other colours from the spectrum except the blue. The military are studying this process; the ability to control light reflection would provide the ultimate camouflage for a soldier wanting to disappear into his/her environment.

95
Light-reflecting 'muzun' or sequins were incorporated into 'ssmatt', a saddlebag carried by Berber men, to ward off the evil eye.

96
Environmental conditions dictate whether the body is visible or concealed in this Prada raincoat. It is usually transparent but turns opaque when wet.

94
Blue Morpho butterfly
Close-up of wing surface

95
Berber sequins
Detail of ssmatt

96
Prada
Autumn/Winter 2002

Professor Yoel Fink, a materials scientist working at MIT's Institute for Soldier Nanotechnologies, has developed a *photonic bandgap fibre*, which has a highly reflective surface. This 'mirror fibre' could enable soldiers to distinguish friend from foe when woven into a fabric. Using *infrared* goggles, which would pick up part of the light spectrum invisible to the naked eye, the fabric could be read like a barcode. In addition, by adjusting the thickness of the thread with an electrical charge, the reflective properties could be altered so the fibre would protect the wearer from radiation, or provide camouflage by changing colour.

The most likely technological route to a real cloth display will be from a specially engineered light-emitting *polymer*. Scientists are working on dynamic colour-changing chameleon fibres.[9] These are essentially hollow conductive fibres with an *electrochromic* coating, which, when the electrode core is charged, turn colour (light) on and off. A team headed by Professor Richard Gregory at Old Dominion University in Virginia intends to integrate these fibres into woven, knitted and possibly even non-woven fabrics. Reporting in a 2003 scientific journal, Professor Gregory and co-author Stephen Hardaker claimed that 'the age of smart, colour-changing fibre and fabric systems may be just around the corner.'[10]

...fashion as software

Evidently, the fashion industry will only start to engage with textile displays when the aesthetic potential matches the functional promise. However, once a cloth display becomes commercially viable it will cause a revolution in the fashion world. If a fabric can be wiped and rewritten with a fresh image, like a computer screen, what would be the need for textile designers? And, more importantly, what would be the need for

97
The Invisible Man films were based on H.G. Wells's 1897 science-fiction novel of that name. Always ahead of his time, Wells understood that the key to invisibility lay in the refraction and reflection of light. His character Griffin, a scientist who discovers the key to invisibility, explains: 'So little suffices to make us visible one to the other. For the most part the fibres of a living creature are no more opaque than water.'

98
This advertisement shows outfits designed half in regular textiles and half in cellophane to demonstrate the fit of underwear. Future clothing may be transparent when supplied so that colour and pattern can be downloaded.

97
The Invisible Man Returns, 1940

98
Half-and-half attire, 1939

more than one garment in that shape? Textile designers may soon be required to reinvent themselves and seasonal print collections could become obsolete. Instead, consumers might access a designer's or brand's online portfolio to download new collections of surface design into their 'digital' garment as and when they chose.

Could fashion itself become a virtual product? Will it disappear as *softwear* and emerge as *software*? Certainly, colour and pattern could be expressed using software. Alongside Microsoft Windows 2012 for our home computer we might purchase Nike Olympic Edition 2012 for our running gear. Other software packages might provide design tools for anyone to programme their own wearable visuals. Once individuals have access to such democratic technological design tools, the structure of the fashion industry will be radically redefined.

The language of clothes is sophisticated and the reasons for buying them myriad, the result of subconscious as much as deliberate choice. There is so much more to fabric and fashion than just colour and pattern; texture, weight, drape, finish, quality, fit, shape, washability, durability, breathability and branding are all factors in what we decide to buy. One fabric fits all will not wipe out the need for fashion and textile designers overnight. But when fashion has reached the point of moving so fast that it has attained a kind of stasis, what is left but to make the garment itself changeable? Being able to update it with a fresh look, just like one might buy a new ringtone for a mobile phone, could make customizability the ultimate selling point. Fashion may indeed be reduced to the binary 'ones and zeroes' of machine code.

99
With a little digital assistance, Mike Thomas's shoot renders the Hussein Chalayan outfit on the model invisible. Chameleon camouflage would turn this idea into a reality.

100
Professor Susumu Tachi of the University of Tokyo demonstrated the principle of optical camouflage with his 'transparent' coat. A masked object has a background image (captured with a video camera) projected onto it. This makes it appear transparent and the viewer is fooled into thinking they are seeing 'through' the wearer. The art of camouflage is to make the garment and its wearer mimic their immediate environment so that one becomes indistinguishable from the other.

101
In this collection, Naoki Takizawa played with the viewer's perception of colour, shape and form. These delicate floral patterns, when viewed from a distance, confuse the eye, camouflaging garment details and accessories.

99
Dazed & Confused
The Difference is Clear, 1998

100
Professor Susumu Tachi
Transparent coat, 2003

101
Naoki Takizawa for Issey Miyake
Spring/Summer 2003

CHAPTER
FIVE /
THE
GLOWING
BALLGOWN

hussein
chalayan
2001

For me technology essentially broadens my language as a designer. I'm interested in languages that allow you to go beyond consideration of the body or 'normal' clothing to create new ways of looking. The importance of technology in my work is that it presents a fresh means of expression.

102
Diana Dew
Electroluminescent dress, 1966

The appeal of light-reflecting clothing and adornment is almost as old as civilization itself. On the most primitive level, the eye delights in the glitter of light on surfaces and the magical transformation of materials. But for many cultures throughout history light and its sources have also been powerful symbols of life, divinity and hope, often becoming the subject of religious worship. In ritual dress, light is used to convey the wearer's status as well as to communicate to higher spiritual powers – Haitian shamans, for example, use light-flashing tunics to summon their gods. Central American, Middle Eastern and Asian cultures all share the belief that light-reflecting textiles ward off evil spirits. Shine, gloss and luminescence also have a long association with wealth and prosperity – early sequins were actually coins and nomadic tribes found that sewing them into their clothing was the easiest way of transporting their wealth.[1] Reflective cloths and body embellishments may have a long tradition, but the ability to emit light from and through dress is a relatively new phenomenon. To date, only a few fashion designers have experimented with this type of clothing.

102
'Light-up' clubbing fashions were created by 1960s avant-garde American designer Diana Dew. Her battery-operated garments had inserted panels of electroluminescent film that flashed rhythmically in time with music. Her clothes were sold in the cult New York boutique Paraphernalia.

103
Dozens of battery-powered coloured LEDs were embedded in a moulded transparent acrylic bodice for McQueen's futuristic Givenchy collection. It was worn with photo-luminescent circuitboard print trousers.

104/105
Japanese jeweller and light artist Erina Kashihara creates wearable light ornaments using LEDs and motion sensors. As the wearer moves so the lights fluctuate, painting the body's movements in the air.

...lyrical light

During the 1990s the British conceptual fashion-designer Hussein Chalayan investigated the application of artificial light in fashion. For part of Chalayan's Spring/Summer 1995 collection, entitled 'Temporary Interference', he expressed religious themes using light within dress:

The idea sprang from the Enlightenment. My use of light was to represent the point of ecstasy in the religious union with God, God as light – light after all gives life to everything. I wanted to work with different tones of light. The use of two distinct light-emitting materials was meant to suggest a flame immediately around the body, and a

103
Alexander McQueen for Givenchy
Autumn/Winter 1999/2000

104
Erina Kashihara
Light Extension, 1993

105
Erina Kashihara
Misty Wind, 1993

softer glow outside – like in religious iconography where a saint is bathed in a pool of holy light. Back then – pre fibre-optic fabrics and electrically powered materials – this was the only way I could achieve this effect. I also wanted the clothes to look like they were floating, like ghosts. You couldn't really see the models' head and hands, just a kind of floating, illuminated body.[2]

Jackets were constructed from a *photoluminescent* rubber material that stores light from conventional sources, whether daylight or electrical lighting, and then glows in the dark. Chalayan's models were hugged backstage in bright light; hands, arms and bodies masked areas of the garments. When they exited onto the dark runway, all the audience could see were glowing clothes imprinted with the echoes of absent human contact. The flowing undergarments were smeared with what appeared to be 'liquid' light. For this Chalayan used light sticks. These tubes contain two chemical compounds, one of which is stored in a very thin capsule. Bending or flexing the stick causes the capsule to break and light is produced by the chemicals mixing, a process known as *chemiluminescence*. This 'liquid' light was 'wiped' onto garments just before each model came out. Using these various materials, Chalayan explored and expanded clothing's capacity for creative communication.

The following season, as part of his Autumn/Winter 1995 collection 'Along False Equator', Chalayan integrated tiny *light-emitting diodes* (LEDs) in jackets printed with holographic flight paths. The LEDs were programmed to sparkle in a sequence that suggested not only the global passage of human traffic, but also the individual's journey through life. The body as a site to be explored is a recurrent theme in the designer's work. Chalayan's subsequent projects have extended to play with light

98

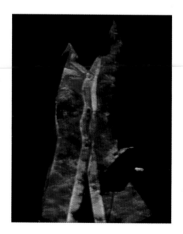

106
Hussein Chalayan
Autumn/Winter 1995

107
Naomi Filmer for Hussein Chalayan
Mouth Light, Spring/Summer 1996

108
Hussein Chalayan
Spring/Summer 1995

109
Hussein Chalayan
Spring/Summer 1995

as a painterly medium. In 2002, as guest editor and curator of *C* magazine, he collaborated on a photo-shoot with the British photographer Nick Knight, using coloured light projections as a form of make-up on a nude face.[3]

Similarly, light projections have also been employed to 'dress' buildings, making temporary but flamboyant architectural gestures. Light is increasingly becoming a creative medium in its own right. Jane Pavitt, the curator of the 2004 exhibition entitled 'Brilliant' at the Victoria and Albert Museum in London, described new technologies such as LEDs and fibre optics as opening up exciting new 'lyrical potentials for light in design'. Pavitt identifies a trend towards a 'blurring of the boundaries between product design and other disciplines, such as fashion and textiles as well as fine art. Although not strictly lighting, the incorporation of light technologies into fabrics is a current avenue of exploration that cannot be ignored.'[4]

...electric jewels

The union of electricity and light in fashion is not exclusively a twentieth-century phenomenon. Battery-powered 'flash jewellery', in the form of kinetic or illuminated hatpins, brooches and diadems, became a fashion fad in France and England during the late 1870s and 1880s.[5] The journals *La Nature* and *Scientific American* documented the designs of Monsieur Trouvé in Paris, labelled Electric Jewels, to be worn in the costumes of dancers and stage performers. They were powered by 2–4 volt hidden batteries and operated by a switch carried in a pocket. Glass gemstones placed over tiny bulbs accented the sparkling electric magic so that, as *Electric World* commented, 'a dashing *demi-mondaine* can thus make a pennyworth of glass eclipse a duchess's diamonds or rubies.'[6]

110
In New York in 1883, the wealthy American socialite Mrs Cornelius Vanderbilt graced her sister-in-law's lavish masquerade ball attired in a design by the couturier of the day, Charles Frederick Worth. Her costume was entitled *Spirit of Electricity* and the sparkle of her diamond-studded headdress was reportedly illuminated further by tiny light bulbs powered by a hidden battery. The dress was pale yellow and shell-pink satin embroidered with tinsel, gilt and silver thread, and the train was Prussian-blue velvet embroidered with gold.

111/112
Two late nineteenth-century engravings from the scientific journal *La Nature*. Then, as now, powering wearable electronics was an issue. *La Nature* noted: 'These trinkets will surely win great popularity, especially in the cities where ample facilities exist for charging small accumulators.'

110
Mrs Cornelius Vanderbilt
Spirit of Electricity, 1883

111
Monsieur Trouvé
Electric Jewels, 1884

112
Monsieur Trouvé
Electric Jewels, 1884

In 2003, over a hundred and twenty years after Trouvé created his 'artificial gems', the *Washington Post* reported:

New Age sophisticates seemed destined to light up at the gift of Moi, a battery powered, wearable electronic jewel. For a mere $25 it offered the sparkle of a green, amber or white light-emitting diode at the end of a wrap-around wire, which makes diamonds irrelevant.[7]

Created by Despina Papadopoulos, founder of the New York based company 5050 Ltd, Moi is simply an LED on a fine wire with a custom-made battery clip. Papadopoulos decided to take this basic electronic element and treat it as something precious, allowing wearers to decide for themselves what it could be. She states:

Moi is not a bracelet or necklace or hair-tie although it could be all of those things…I'm fascinated by the uses people find for it; when we were developing it people would say to us 'you should put instructions on the packet, you should have drawings that show people how to use it/wear it'. And I said no (!) absolutely not, because the whole idea is that you give people a piece of string and they'll do with it whatever they want.[8]

Moi seems to encourage social exchanges. In Papadopoulos's own experience 'almost everyone will comment on it to the point where, if I don't feel in an outgoing mood, I leave it at home…If you exhibit a certain behaviour that attracts attention then you are fair game for people to come and talk to you. You are, after all, wearing a bright light!'[9] Some enquire whether it is powered by the wearer's heart, keen to invest some greater significance in this minimal light. Nonetheless, 5050 believe Moi is an

113
5050's simple LED Moi is marketed as: 'A wearable electronic radiant light device. A sparkle. A moment of magic. Wear it, hold it, give it. Moi is for you to do as you please.'

114
Using LEDs, fabric circuitry, a battery and sensors, Maggie Orth's Firefly dress senses motion and lights up when the wearer is in close proximity to other people.

115
Ulli Oberlack is a jewelry PhD student at Central Saint Martins College of Art & Design in London. She is interested in light as body adornment and works with LEDs, batteries and mixed media to illuminate the body with wearable light projections.

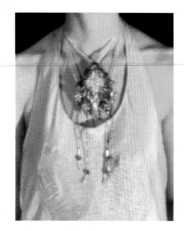 

113
5050
Moi, 2003

114
Maggie Orth
Firefly necklace and dress, 1997

115
Ulli Oberlack
Travelling Light, 2003

indication of what consumers may be ready to adopt in terms of wearable technology. As we are people living increasingly isolated lives, we may come to regard such products as ice-breakers inviting social interaction.

...printable light

Clothing capable of mediating relationships between people and with our environment is a persistent theme in technology circles. The American Elise Co, an alumna of the Aesthetics and Computation Group at the MIT Media Laboratory, has produced an environmentally sensitive raincoat called the Puddlejumper. Rain sensors embroidered on the back of the jacket are wired to silk-screened *electroluminescent* (EL) lamps on the front. When it rains the lamps shine. The EL patches consist of phosphor ink that emits light when an alternating current is applied. In addition to the playful juxtaposition of electricity and water, Puddlejumper explores the creative potential for integrated technologies. By hiding the mechanical aspects of technology or making them decorative, we are left to focus on the more expressive possibilities. Co, who developed an interest in computer science and technology as part of her architectural training, is the first to admit her device may need some refining when it comes to fashion:'it's nowhere near as sophisticated in execution as a high-fashion garment would be.'[10] EL requires high voltage to glow brightly, making the coat unsuitable to wear at present – it would give a whole new meaning to 'shock value' in fashion.

The ornamental and expressive aspects of EL can also be seen in the work of the British textile-designer Rachel Wingfield. Since 2002, Wingfield has produced a series of reactive products using *sensors*, simple controlling units and EL technology. Light Sleeper comprises pillows and a duvet containing EL wire that glows in the dark and

116/119
Elise Co's electroluminescent raincoat lights up when it starts to rain and an electroluminescent pattern of leaves on Rachel Wingfield's window blind seem to gradually glow and grow as natural daylight subsides. Rachel Wingfield trained as a textile designer but has learnt about electronics and technology to further her creative ambitions; Elise Co emanates from a programming background and taught herself garment skills. There is a trend for design practitioners trained in one discipline to migrate to another, in order to push the boundaries of one or both fields. This emerging pattern of working will inform the design of future creative technology products.

103

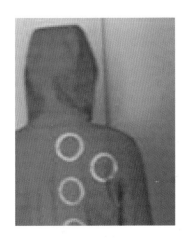

116
Elise Co
Puddlejumper, 2000

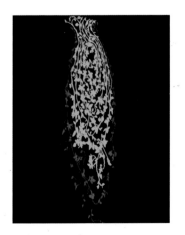

117
Elise Co
Puddlejumper, 2000

118
Rachel Wingfield
Digital Dawn, 2002

119
Rachel Wingfield
Digital Dawn, 2002

can be programmed to illuminate gradually. By mimicking sunrise the sleeper is woken in a natural, pleasant way instead of by a violent alarm. A similar philosophy was applied to Digital Dawn, a light-reactive window blind. As the natural daylight dims, the blind comes to life with a foliage pattern that appears to 'grow and evolve…digitally emulating the process of photosynthesis'[11] and which fluctuates with the changing light levels. Wingfield's work demonstrates how a thoughtful union of design and technology can make for magical effects and might even have emotional and psychological consequences. Applied to fashion, we can imagine 'intelligent' garments, such as day-to-evening wear that senses low light levels and comes to life as the sun sets.

…living light

For the moment it appears that any emission of light in clothing will be created by electricity. Textile research, however, suggests a future where the incorporation of genetically engineered light-emitting bacteria will make *bioactive* fabrics glow.

There are many light-producing organisms on Earth, from squid and fireflies to glow-worms and plankton. Biotechnologists are now harnessing light-emitting bacteria, which generate the enzyme luciferase responsible for producing *bioluminescence*, and introducing them into fibres.[11] Some natural fibres such as milkweed and cotton have a hollow core that can be filled with these bacteria and a growth nutrient. The bacteria feed on the nutrient and emit light for the duration of their lifespan. These fibres can be woven or knitted into fabrics. Other techniques being explored are poly-laminate fabrics where glowing bacteria are loaded into an internal fabric layer that is sandwiched between vapour-permeable outer shells to create the first biologically active glow-in-the-dark fabric.

104

120/122
Atsuko Tanaka, a member of the famous Japanese avant-garde Gutai group of the 1950s and 1960s, created the Electric Dress from flashing coloured light bulbs and neon light tubes, all connected by a mass of cables. The dress combined the traditional kimono with modern industrial technology and Tanaka wore it for a performance happening during the 2nd Gutai Art Exhibition at Ohara Kaikan Hall, Tokyo in October 1956.

120
Atsuko Tanaka
Drawing for Electric Dress, 1956

121
Atsuko Tanaka
Electric Dress, 1956

122
Atsuko Tanaka
Reconstructed Electric Dress, 1986

Many issues remain unresolved in the production of fashion that glows. As with all clothing that requires electricity to function, how to power a garment efficiently and safely is a key concern. In addition, what will stop such an invention from being dismissed simply as a passing fad or gimic? Such clothing will either have to offer new practical functions or, if purely decorative, be subtle and sophisticated in its use of technology. It will require the poetry of the designer to realize the vision of the scientist. Cloth, traditionally used to diffuse light in the home, could be used in the same way on the body. And just as domestic lighting shapes the spaces we inhabit, so body lighting might shape us, highlighting bone structure and creating silhouettes that sculpt the figure.

Clothing that glows in the dark has many potential safety applications – cyclists and runners already use clothing with reflective panels in order to be noticed. But on a broader level, the desire to be made visible through dress is at the very heart of fashion and fabric design. The ability to create light in clothing potentially extends the language of fashion as a form of non-verbal communication. The new dynamic skins offered by sensing and reactive light technologies will enable clothing that mimics nature to signal, warn or attract others. Emotional clothing might glow red to indicate that we do not wish to be disturbed, or a future 'Oscar' dress may bathe an actress in shimmering golden sparkles as she steps onto the red carpet. Light-emitting effects in fashion may dramatically increase the capacity of designers to feed our continuing fascination for clothes that glitter and glow.

123
This jellyfish is probably the most influential bioluminescent marine organism. It is the source of photoproteins and green fluorescent proteins (GFP) that have been cloned for implanting into other living organisms to illuminate growth patterns. The image does not show bioluminescence – it shows a strobe light reflected off the jellyfish. Bioluminescence is not continuous and shows up in the dark as a ring of small green lights around the rim of the bell.

124
Commissioned by the National Maritime Museum in Greenwich, London, where it is on permanent exhibition at 'Rank and Style', Taylor's glove is designed to produce intermittent colour effects. The thumb section lights independently as well as in conjunction with the main body of the glove. It is constructed from nylon monofilament and polymer optical fibre, and the light source is tungsten halide.

125/126
Luminex is a fibre-optic fabric that emits its own light. It can be woven with a mixture of almost any yarns but requires a battery to operate it. Luminex is the result of a collaboration between CAEN SpA, an Italian hi-tech microelectronics company involved in the aerospace industry, and the Swiss textile company Stabio Textile SA.

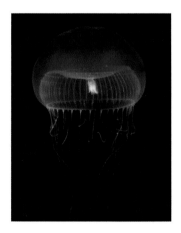

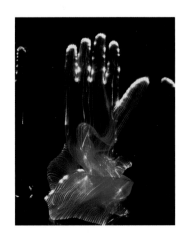

123
Hydromedusa *Aequorea victoria*

124
Sarah Taylor
Woven fibre-optic glove, 1999

125
Luminex
Glowing wedding dress, 2002

126
Luminex
Luminex cloth, 2002

CHAPTER SIX/
THE SHAPE-SHIFTING SKIRT

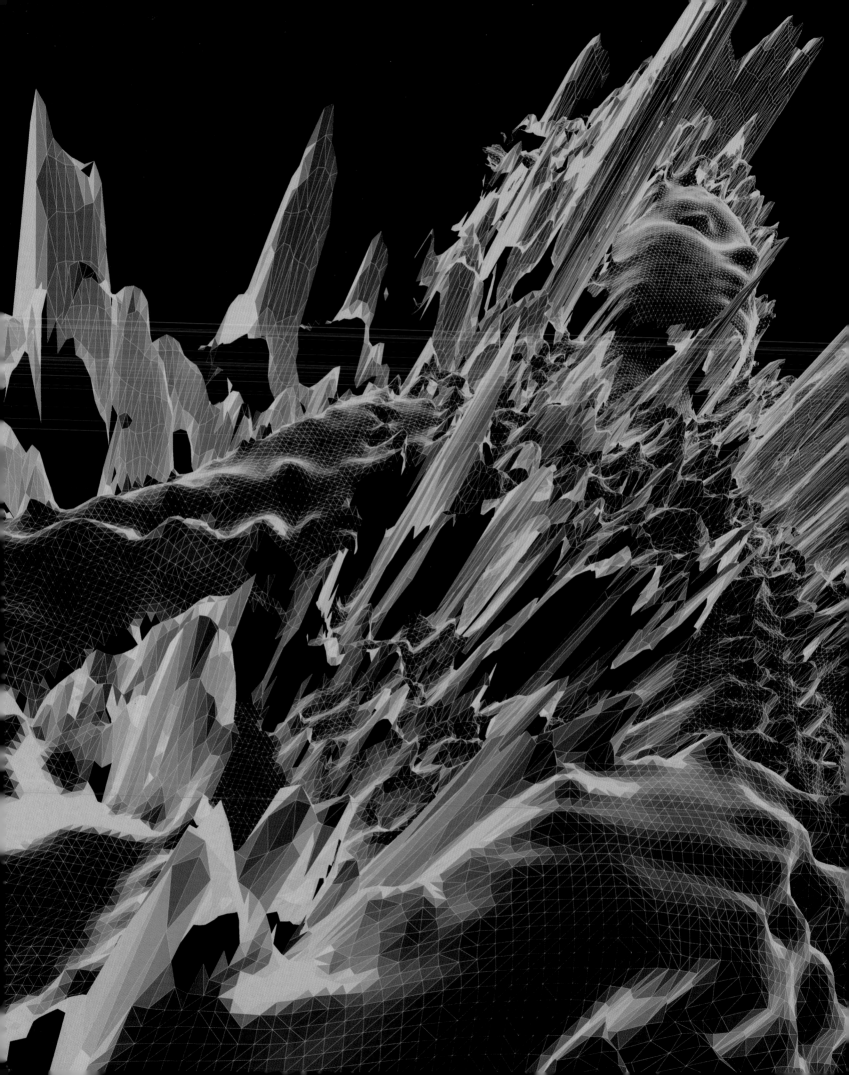

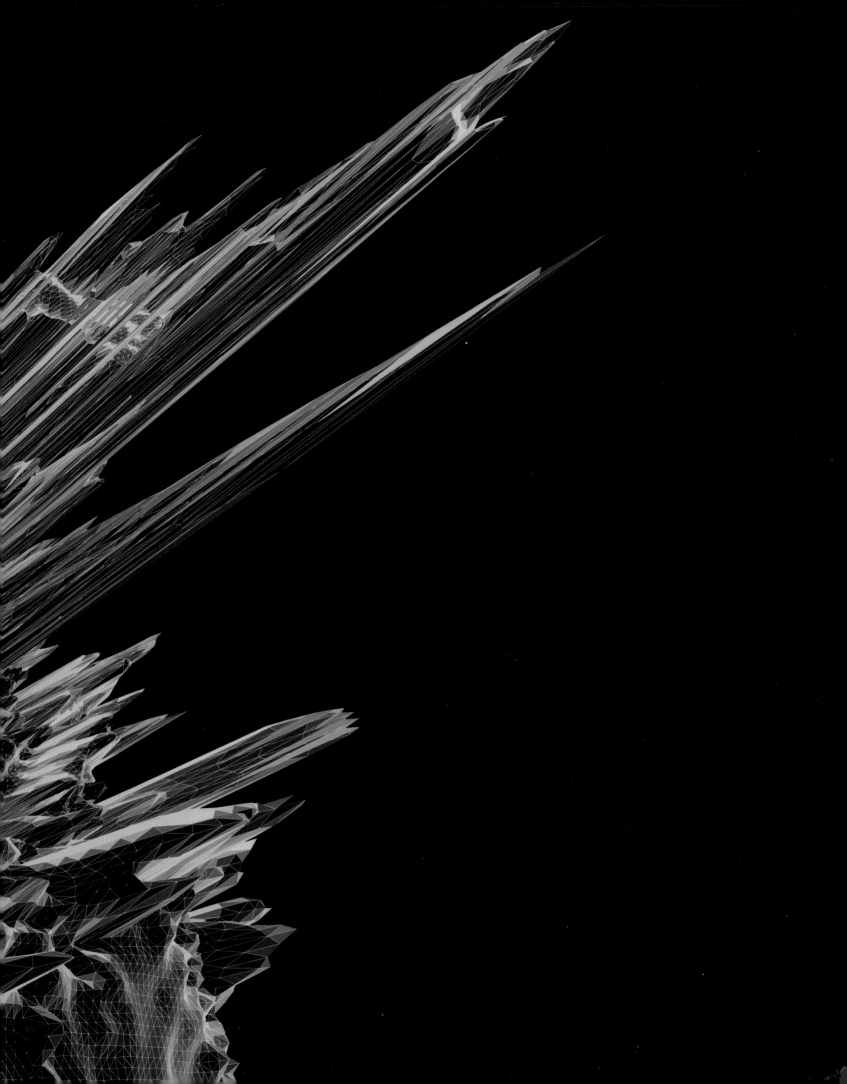

giacomo balla & fortunato depero 1915

The need to vary the environment frequently, together with sport, led us to the concept of TRANSFORMABLE CLOTHES (mechanical trimmings, surprises, tricks, disappearance of individuals).

LE VÊTEMENT MASCULIN
FUTURISTE
Manifeste

L'humanité a toujours porté le deuil, ou l'armure pesante, ou la chape hiératique, ou le manteau traînant. Le corps de l'homme a toujours été attristé par le noir, ou emprisonné de ceintures ou écrasé par des draperies.

Durant le Moyen-Âge et la Renaissance l'habillement a presque toujours eu des couleurs et des formes statiques, pesantes, drapées ou bouffantes, solennelles, graves, sacerdotales, incommodes et encombrantes. C'étaient des expressions de mélancolie, d'esclavage ou de terreur. C'était la négation de la vie musculaire, qui étouffait dans un passéisme anti-hygiénique d'étoffes trop lourdes et de demi-teintes ennuyeuses efféminées ou décadentes.

C'est pourquoi aujourd'hui comme autrefois les rues pleines de foule, les théâtres, et les salons ont une tonalité et un rythme désolants, funéraires et déprimants.

Nous voulons donc abolir:

1. — Les vêtements de deuil que les croque-morts eux-mêmes devraient refuser.

2. — Toutes les couleurs fanées, jolies, neutres, fantaisie, foncées.

3. — Toutes les étoffes à raies, quadrillées et à petits pois.

4. — Les soi-disants bon goût et harmonie de teintes et de formes qui ramollissent les nerfs et ralentissent le pas.

5. — La symétrie dans la coupe, la ligne statique qui fatigue, déprime, contriste, enchaîne les muscles, l'uniformité des revers et toutes les bizarreries ornementales.

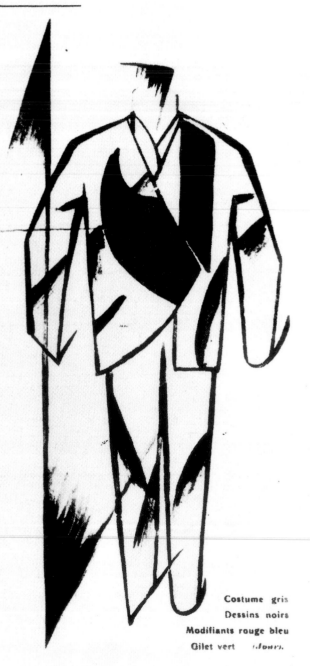

Costume gris
Dessins noirs
Modifiants rouge bleu
Gilet vert   (Jours).

127
Giacomo Balla
'Male Futurist Dress: A Manifesto', 1913–14

The changing of shapes and silhouettes has been one of the defining principles of fashion. Historically, dressmakers and tailors have engineered complex garments in order to modify and constrain the human body. From boning in corsetry to spandex 'control' panels in contemporary lingerie, fashion design has often embraced new technologies to help sculpt the human form. Fashion has, at times, questioned the notion that clothing should retain a constant silhouette, offering instead modular garments that are adaptable to the wearer's situation. Designers have extended the function of clothing by borrowing concepts from, for example, luggage design or portable architecture to create mutable garments that expand, inflate, collapse or flat-pack. In the 'supermodern wardrobe',¹ jackets turn into bags, coats convert into chairs and tables become skirts.

The Italian Futurist movement of the early twentieth century advocated clothing that escaped the fripperies of fashion, proposing, among other things, 'dynamic', 'functional' dress that freed the wearer. In 1914 Giacomo Balla suggested a series of dress 'modifiers' that would enable anyone to 'not only modify but also invent a new dress for a new mood at any instant'. Similarly, in the 1935 manifesto 'Latin Pleasures for the Mind', Filippo Tommaso Marinetti sought 'tactile resonant metaphorical dress tuned to the hour, the day, the season and the mood to convey sensations of dawn, noon, evening, spring, summer, winter, autumn, ambition, love, etc.'

The Futurist vision was radical – to involve the wearer in the finished look of a garment. According to the art historian Radu Stern:

Dress was no longer a given object to which its owner had to submit. The responsibility for controlling changes in dress was given instead to its wearer, who had to enter the

127/128
In 'Male Futurist Dress: A Manifesto', Italian Futurist artist Giacomo Balla presented how a suit might be customized by the wearer according to his mood. He designed a series of cloth 'modifiers' that could change a garment's surface decoration. 'Transformable clothes' were also described in another manifesto, 'The Futurist Reconstruction of the Universe', published by Balla together with fellow Futurist Fortunato Depero. Shape-changing polymers may finally realize the metamorphosing dress envisaged by the Italian Futurists.

129
In 1939, in answer to American *Vogue*'s brief to forecast the future of fashion, Raymond Loewy, more famous for designing trains and automobiles, presented an adaptable dress for day and evening wear. He correctly predicted that in the future people would travel more: 'A New York businesswoman, for instance, may decide on a hurried trip to California...She will want to travel light and...instead of taking along both a day and dinner dress, she may wear a garment that can be readily converted into one or the other.' He proposed a day dress in lightweight wool with sleeves that could be removed for the evening. The outfit was completed by a skullcap with a rotating Polaroid visor 'that can be out of the way, fitted snugly against the crown of the hat, or lowered in front to the eyes to eliminate all glare.'

128
Giacomo Balla
Man's evening suit, 1914

129
Raymond Loewy
All-Hour Dress, 1939

aesthetic realm and collaborate with the designer. Within the limits fixed by the artist, the wearers of clothing could express their own creativity, and in this way attire became an 'open' work of art.[2]

The advent of smart textiles enables the realization of some of those early Futurist dreams, along with all sorts of new, previously unimaginable visions for fabrics and fashion.

...smart shape-shifters

The word 'smart' is applied to a range of materials that react dramatically to external stimuli, changing their properties, structure, composition or function. Smart materials transform with the application of electric current, heat, light, pressure or magnetic forces, changing shape, colour, size or molecular structure (from liquid to solid, etc.). They can be active or passive and often form part of a *smart system* that may be used in design to increase performance or add functions.

Types of smart materials include *shape-memory* alloys (SMAs), *magneto-rheological materials* (MR), *electro-rheostatic materials* (ER), *piezoelectric materials* (PZT) and *electroactive polymers* (EAPs). Smart materials often function as *sensors* and *actuators*, detecting what is happening around them and modifying themselves accordingly. So far, these materials have been embedded in products such as cars and electronic instruments; they have yet to play a role in fashion. Researchers are now exploring ways of engineering fibres and fabrics from these materials to provide new possibilities for function and creativity in fashion. Future clothes made from smart materials will be able to alter shape on a micro-level, with dynamic cloth surfaces that switch state as needed,[3] or at a macro-level by enabling an entire silhouette to change.

116

130
Two women in Hyde Park demonstrate springs strapped to shoes. They were believed to help exercise the legs. Today, sports-shoe manufacturers build spring action into soles. Adidas 1s, released in December 2004, were described as 'intelligent trainers': they use electronics developed by Motorola to sense the wearer's activity and then adjust inflatable air bladders to support and cushion the feet as necessary.

131
A woman hangs out the washing that she is carrying in an inflatable basket section of her apron. Heat-sealed and welded rubber and plastic have been used over the decades to create inflatable garments adaptable to changing circumstances.

132/133
In his 'Before Minus Now' collection Chalayan showed a remote-controlled dress to imply that intangible forces were at work. The hard resin shell suddenly opened to expose a cloud of pink tulle.

130
Spring shoes, 1930

131
Inflatable carrier/apron, 1956

132
Hussein Chalayan
Spring/Summer 2000

133
Hussein Chalayan
Spring/Summer 2000

We already take for granted some smart materials that are used in the fashion industry. For example, the under-wires in modern bras, which are designed to return to their original shape after being in the washing machine, and spectacles that can be crumpled and squashed but spring back into shape, are both fabricated from SMAs. The most widely used SMAs, known as *Nitinol*, are fabricated from nickel-titanium and can 'remember' their original shape.

'Memory' materials come in the form of metals, *polymers*, plastics, even gels. They can be stimulated in different ways – by electricity, heat, magnetism or chemicals. For his Spring/Summer 'Before Minus Now' collection of 2000, the designer Hussein Chalayan created a prom dress with a shape-changing skirt. With electrically triggered 'memory' wire sewn into the garment's hem, the flick of a switch could turn a softly draping silhouette into a pert party frock. Although a mains power supply was required to trigger the change (making it a show effect rather than a viable ready-to-wear garment), it was the first high-fashion demonstration of shape-change technology's potential.

Shape-memory metals have been around since the late 1930s but research is increasingly focused on shape-memory polymers (SMPs). SMPs work under a wider range of conditions than SMAs and are capable of even more dramatic shape-change. Used within the human body as biodegradable self-tying sutures, they are activated upon reaching body temperature or via interaction with a specific chemical compound. In textiles, shape-memory polyurethanes are being harnessed to provide protective clothing for extreme temperatures. Mitsubishi's Diaplex fabric laminates a shape-memory polymer layer, which adapts to external conditions, onto a variety of fashion fabrics. It is simultaneously waterproof and windproof, yet breathable. Other research

134

Italian fashion label Corpo Nove pioneered the use of Nitinol (a thermal shape-memory alloy) in fabric for Oricalco, a shirt that changes shape as it gets hot. The thermal shape-memory alloy is characterized by its extraordinary ability to recover any pre-programmed shape upon heating. Until now, this lightweight alloy, made with about 50 per cent titanium, has been used in high-tech industries like space and medicine. With help from the European Space Agency (ESA), Corpo Nove's research arm, Grado Zero Espace, integrated Nitinol into a fabric from which they manufactured a long-sleeved shirt. It meant that the creased garment could be taken out of a suitcase and with a blast of hot air from a hairdryer, the shape-memory yarns would relax back to their smooth former state. And the sleeves were 'programmed' to shorten immediately the room temperature became a few degrees hotter.

135/136

In his 'Beforre Minus Now' collection, Hussein Chalayan challenged gravity by sewing shape-changing memory wire into the hem of a dress, which, when electrically activated, lifted and spread the skirt as if it was held by some invisible force-field.

134
Corpo Nove
Shape-memory shirt, 2000

135
Hussein Chalayan
Spring/Summer 2000

136
Hussein Chalayan
Spring/Summer 2000

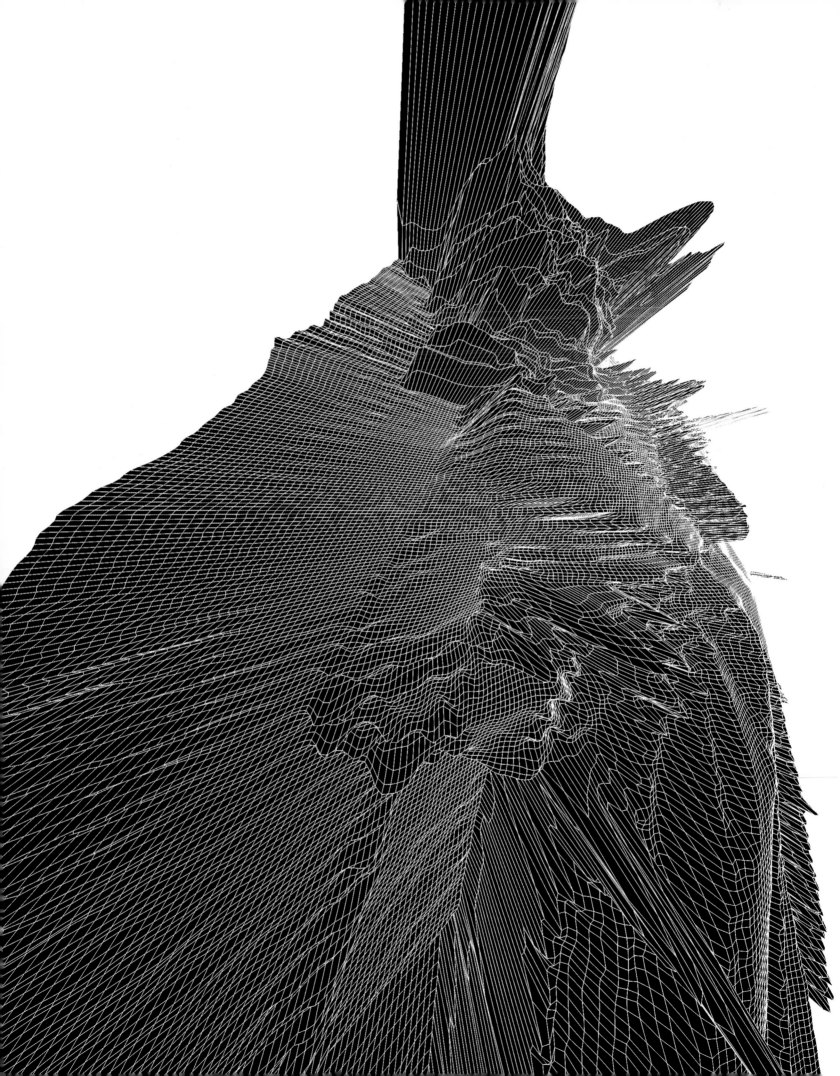

includes shape-memory springs that are sandwiched between layers of fabric. When exposed to heat, the springs open out, pushing the internal and external fabric layers apart to create insulation for fire-fighters.

Clearly functional applications for SMP-based textiles abound, but what of the aesthetic potential? Imagine tight weaves that open to become floppy and draped, knits that flip from knobbly to smooth, fake furs that fluff up like a bird's feathers in harsh wind or icy temperatures and then relax to silky sleek with indoor warmth. Perhaps garments will iron themselves, or remember our preferred fit — new jeans that instantly mould to the wearer's curves as if they'd been worn for ten years.

...magnetic mode

For his 1993 graduation collection at Central Saint Martins College of Art & Design in London, Hussein Chalayan concealed magnets in the hems of skirts and dresses as well as the runway's surface, making clothes 'snap' into different shapes. The clothes gave the impression of being pulled by an invisible force-field — Chalayan was using magnetism for shape-shifting fashion. Until now, magnetism in fashion has been limited to invisible fasteners on clothing or closures for bags. But for clothes really to change shape we may need to look for more high-tech solutions. Researchers are now exploring the potential use of magneto-rheological (MR) and *ferromagnetic* fluids in fabrics that can be flexible one second and rigid the next. In a project funded by the US Army, Dr Gareth McKinley and his team at MIT's Institute for Soldier Nanotechnologies are attempting to make instant armour for soldiers that would become bulletproof at the flick of a switch. MR and ferromagnetic fluids contain nanoparticles of iron oxide. When placed near a magnetic field the particles instantly organize themselves into a solid, and when removed they revert back to their original flowing state. The fluid could be

137
Belgian designer Van Beirendonck is fascinated by the applications of new technology in fashion and for the human body. He has explored themes of cloning and the idea of artificially extending the body. The vinyl Killer jacket for his W&LT (Wild and Lethal Trash) line was designed to reshape the body – in place of vigorous workouts it encouraged the wearer just to blow up their 'muscles' using nozzles like those on a pool toy.

138
This bright blue polyurethane inflatable jacket is one of a series of transformable garments designed by CP Company. It came with an air pump to turn it into an armchair.

139/140
In this collection, Japanese designer Naoki Takizawa presented a water-proof parka neatly packed into a collar/harness; it could be unfurled in the event of a sudden downpour.

137
Walter Van Beirendonck
Killer jacket, 1996

138
CP Company
Jacket/armchair, 2001

139
Naoki Takizawa for Issey Miyake
Spring/Summer 2005

140
Naoki Takizawa for Issey Miyake
Spring/Summer 2005

contained in fine rubber tubing woven into a fabric or a fabric could be saturated with the fluid and sealed with plastic sheeting. McKinley explains that by controlling the application of a magnetic field the fabric could change from soft and flexible to rigid, as the field gets stronger. This would provide a protection system of adjustable strength.[4]

The magnetic field in a piece of clothing would probably be electrically activated, which would enable the wearer to control the function. The researchers at MIT are focused on this technology's military applications, but in the long-term, if the powering method can be resolved (it does require substantial power, which is a drawback for a wearable system), it may well filter down to the apparel market. MR materials might be incorporated into sports or protective clothing. 'Polar' clothing may take on a whole new meaning -- of the magnetic, not Arctic, variety. North and south might signal relaxed or alert modes. If anxious when walking home alone at night, the wearer might choose to activate an 'armoured garment' mode, turning a soft, puffa jacket into an attack-resistant body shell. Another vision might be for fashion that can change from casual to formal.

McKinley's team don't expect to have instant bulletproof armour for at least ten years, and we may have to wait a good deal longer for a fashion version to be perfected. Imagine what would happen if you unintentionally sashayed past a strong magnetic field dressed in your magnetic ensemble.

...electric threads

One of the most discussed drivers for future smart textiles and clothing is a category of materials known as electroactive polymers (EAPs). Also known as intelligent or conducting polymers, and often called 'artificial muscles', EAPs change shape or size when an electric charge is applied. Just like real muscles, these polymers can bend

141/144

Mystique, Cute Circuit's shape-shifting dress, is a time-based garment that changes shape and length in the course of an evening. Initially, the dress is pale grey, knee length and has a soft padded surface; by the end of the night it has become long and smooth, revealing a new colour. The dress is a double-face silk cylinder that is grey when folded inside out, and unfolded is bright red with mother-of-pearl embroidery. The software that runs the dress calculates how much time has passed and understands the mood of the wearer, so that in the beginning, when grey, the dress reflects a calm and reserved attitude, and then, as time passes, it unfolds, slowly revealing the wearer's inner nature (more at ease and colourful).

122

141/144
Cute Circuit
Mystique, 2004

142

143

144

and straighten as necessary. The existing array of EAP materials includes gels, rubbers and films, but smart fabric and clothing will require a fibre-like form. EAP technology is forecast to transfer into everyday clothing for wearable computing, personal communication, gaming and medical use. According to the NASA researcher and EAP expert, Yoseph Bar-Cohen:

Using EAP fibres, which can consist of conductive polymers, would enable a new era in clothing and gossamer structures, allowing controlled configuration and shape. EAP fibres can be actuated [triggered] and, while maintaining flexibility, they offer the potential to adjust the thermal insulation of clothing.[5]

Bar-Cohen asserts that it is still very early days in the development of smart fabrics manufactured from EAPs. To achieve this kind of material will require a multi-disciplinary approach, bringing together such diverse fields as electronics, textiles, *materials science* and chemistry. Potentially suited to more diverse uses than SMAs, and with production techniques that may include ink-jet printing or *rapid prototyping*, EAP materials seem set to play an important role in future smart clothes and accessories.

…back to the futurists

Giacomo Balla's fight against 'static' and fixed dress has come of age with the emergence of shape-changing materials. And though we have some way to go before clothes can be 'tuned' to the season or even to love, these artistic desires no longer seem as unobtainable as they once did.

Mutable clothing will find applications in healthcare, the military and the emergency services. Fabrics will adjust their shape – shift in light, close up in cold, erect to

145
The fabric of Cute Circuit's Mystique is embroidered with mother of pearl and small metallic sequins and held in place by small clips controlled by a microprocessor. The clips are placed at various heights and are electrically triggered to detach, allowing the fabric to unfold. When the dress is unfolded the mother-of-pearl petals embroidered around the detachment clips look like flowers.

123

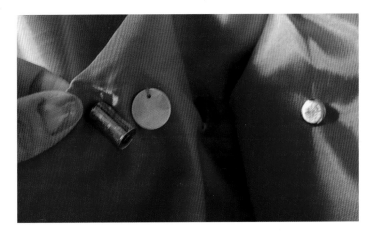

145
Cute Circuit
Mystique, 2004

protect — depending on their composition, enabling a multitude of imaginative uses. Shape-change materials and smart systems will work with the wearer, taking us from formal to casual, from defensive to relaxed. New protective functions for clothing will include cushioning falls for the elderly, relieving back-pain for pregnant women and shielding the vulnerable from street attack. The body-obsessed will no doubt welcome hi-tech corsetry — fabric that sculpts, pinches and squeezes in all the right places to achieve a slimmer silhouette, or garments that can be programmed to support or constrict into a preferred body shape. Shape-change fabrics will be used in the sport, leisure and entertainment industries. EAPs will form the basis of most wearable electronics from programmable jackets and caring camisoles to talking T-shirts.

For any of these ideas to seize the public imagination th   at least as well as traditional ones — they n   hard-wearing and affordable. No small   cality, comfort and invisible technology — ju   le, is less concerned with such issues, bein   etry. The use of the technologies mention   ure. They suggest exciting possibilities for   on designers we can only muse on their c

The acceleration of retro-recycling of sty   ntury might reach its zenith mid-century in fas   eyes. For personal styling a new genre of 'peacoc   accessories, which suddenly burst into extravagant display, can be envisaged. Fashion's vitality thrives on its appropriation and interpretation of different cultures and ethnicities. Smart, mutable clothing might further facilitate individuals to shape trends and create trends for shape.

146/147
Chalayan's celebrated 'After Words' collection featured a room furnished with four chairs and a coffee table. Intended as a comment on war and the plight of refugees who suddenly have to carry all their belongings with them, four models took off the chair covers and transformed them into dresses, and another made the table into a skirt. Finally, the chairs themselves were turned into suitcases.

146
Hussein Chalayan
Autumn/Winter 2000

147
Hussein Chalayan
Autumn/Winter 2000

CHAPTER SEVEN /
THE INSTANT BIKINI

freedom
of
creation
2004

One day we will live in a world where consumer products will be completely tailored for the individual and not the masses...In the same manner as we have water pipelines running into our homes, one day we could have futuristic pipelines that would transport polymers and other compounds that we would run through nano-assemblers (devices for rearranging molecules) to manufacture items of our choice.

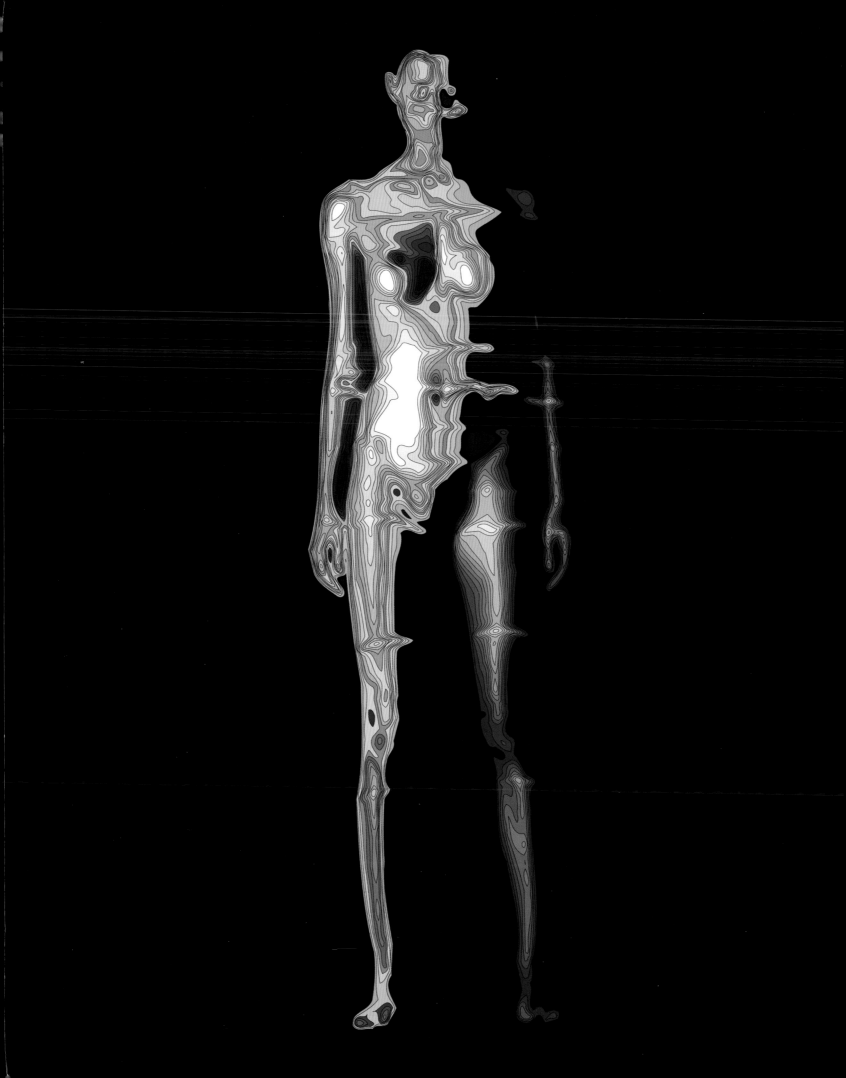

Twenty-first-century research envisages an entirely new method of fashion manufacture that will replace woven fabrics with *3D-printed* fashion. Using technology from the car and product-design industries, researchers are creating individually tailored and uniquely detailed 'instant' garments that are designed in 3D on computer, mapped to 3D-scanned body measurements and 'printed' out. It might be a frock, bag, shoes — whatever you desire. Known as Direct Manufacture or 3D printing, it requires a radical rethink of the fashion industry. Directly manufactured clothing made from powdered *polymers* bonded together with lasers could pose a threat to the sewing machine. No factories, supply chains or even shops as we know them — just powder organized into form by data and lasers. It is a post-industrial vision that has the potential to challenge nineteenth-century patterns of production as well as to re-shape our future desires as consumers.

... techno-bespoke

Direct Manufacture or 3D Printing has grown out of *Rapid Prototyping*, an industrial process for the creation of complex prototypes or moulds.[1] In the same way, we now use desktop printers to print a 2D paper image of a digital file, 3D printers print out physical 3D objects. Rapid Prototyping is used by automotive and aeronautical engineers to test parts, and by sports-shoe manufacturers to try out designs. *Computer-aided design (CAD)* software enables a designer to create a 3D virtual model of a design which can then be exported directly to a 3D printer. A CAD file can be emailed from a design studio in California to a factory in Indonesia, where a prototype shoe can be printed out. Rapid Prototyping generates a model to be mass-produced on a conventional production line, but 3D Printing is now being employed to create a final product. The use of 3D Printing for manufacturing also offers the possibility of making unique one-offs — mass customization.

148/150
The Dutch Museum for Contemporary Art – Het Kruithuis – held a design competition to celebrate the February 2002 wedding of Crown Prince Willem-Alexander and Máxima Zorreguieta. The museum asked 24 designers to create a royal crown for the new princess. The entry from Marcel Wanders's studio was a delicate and crystalline diadem inspired by nature. The design's basic concept came from the effect of a splash of water, an element that has been central to Dutch culture and history. To create this unconventional shape, Wanders employed rapid prototyping technology. A 3D CAD (computer-aided design) model of the crown was converted into an electronic file which could be read by a stereolithography machine that prints models layer by layer. A laser beam traced each layer onto the surface of a vat of photopolymer resin, building the crown in repeated layers until a solid replica of the original CAD model was completed. Prototypes of Wanders's crown were modelled using a 3D printer at the Belgian company Materialise. The final crown was cast in silver.

133

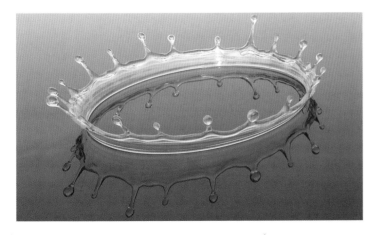

148/150
Marcel Wanders
Water Crown, 2001

149

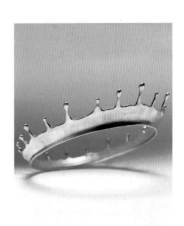

150

Janne Kyttanen and Jiri Evenhuis of the Dutch company Freedom of Creation (FOC) are pioneering the use of 3D print in design. They have created a patent-pending 3D-printed textile that resembles the chainmail fabrics Paco Rabanne created in the 1960s, with one major difference: Rabanne's links were painstakingly crafted by hand; FOC's links have no seams. Indeed, the entire fabric is 'compiled' in one go from nylon powder.

For the most part, 3D design is unfamiliar to the world of high fashion, where, at best, an inspirational sketch and sometimes only a front view is given to a pattern cutter to interpret. To create a 3D printed garment requires a designer not only to think in 3D, but also to engage with a whole new fabric topography. The focus shifts from consideration of darts and seams, now rendered obsolete, to a concern with silhouette and surface – the opportunity exists for the interior and exterior surfaces of a fabric or garment to be radically different. An opening for access is still required, of course, as is a method of fastening – a zip could be created as an integral part of the structure. 3D print presents entirely new functional and aesthetic possibilities. Instead of a fabric having one property, such as transparency, drape, rigidity or stretch, all of these would be possible at once. A designer would not have to layer or seam together fabrics to build shape or volume, but could think in terms of increasing depth or density in certain areas of the garment, a bit like sculpting ridges or valleys. Complex constructions could be effortlessly executed – soft, fluid, organic forms might grow into rigid spikes. This process promises a fresh landscape for experimentation in fashion.

... wearable structures

Philip Delamore, a print designer and Senior Research Fellow at the London College of Fashion, is working with Kyttanen to develop 3D print further for clothing. According to

151/154
Janne Kyttanen and Jiri Evenhuis of Freedom of Creation design their products using CAD and output their 3D files to be rapid manufactured using stereolithography. A garment can be created with an intricate textile structure; the size and shape of the chainmail links can be altered, and moving parts or logos can be integrated and printed out as an individual finished product.

155
French singer Françoise Hardy wore Paco Rabanne's metal chainmail all-in-one for a concert in 1968. Each link was joined by hand and it weighed 16 kilos, taking over an hour to put on. Contemporary rapid-manufacture technology would enable this ensemble to be 'printed' all in one go, including a fully functioning zip.

151
Freedom of Creation
3D printed steel textile

152
Freedom of Creation
3D printed aluminium, steel, nylon

153
Freedom of Creation
3D printed nylon chainmail bag

154
Freedom of Creation
3D printed nylon top, 2004

155
Paco Rabanne
Chainmail suit, 1968

Delamore, there will have to be developments in this technology before it can be used in the fashion industry. The first task is to create a 3D design environment (software) to enable a 3D body-scan to be imported, manipulated and turned into a design that can be outputted to a 3D print machine. Secondly, major advances are required in the field of *materials science* in order to extend the possibilities of printing more fabric-like materials, beyond synthetic polymers like nylon, to organic resources such as cotton, silk or cellulose. More research needs to be done into the processes of integrating stretch and elasticity, and, finally, the printing machines (hardwear) will have to be adapted to cope with the challenge posed by these garments. Delamore is also keen to explore the scope for sustainability. Z Corporation, a leader in 3D-print technology in America, makes machines that create design prototypes using a powder-binder technology. The powder is a plaster- or starch-based material and any unused powder can be recycled. The final object is about fifty per cent porous and can be infiltrated with resins, waxes or urethanes for added strength and durability. Delamore says:

I think that kind of system is quite a desirable model because it would be good to have something which is non-petroleum based. The whole idea with this process is that you don't have to weave fabric or knit cloth, there's no construction, you start with a raw material and you actually build the entire garment. Rather than shipping fabric or clothes around the world you just ship data. It's the opposite of 'think local act global', it's back to 'think global act local'.[2]

A fashion store might have a manufacturing facility in-house so that customers could watch a fashion show, or view sample garments on a rail, and, once they have made a selection, feed in their measurements to have a couture garment printed out on the spot.

156/157
Z Corporation develops, manufactures, and markets the world's fastest 3D printers – machines that produce physical prototypes quickly, easily and inexpensively from CAD and other digital data. In the same way that conventional desktop printers provide computer users with a paper output of their documents, 3D printers provide 3D CAD users with a physical prototype of objects such as mobile phones or shoes. Manufacturers and suppliers of footwear, including athletic, designer and casual shoes, have a real need for concept models to speed up and improve the often rushed design process. Z Corp's 3D colour printer can create full-colour models that facilitate communication about design intent as well as more constructive feedback.

158
For this collection, Naoki Takizawa took inspiration from high-tech sports-shoe styling and manufacturing technology to create a multi-coloured thermoplastic mesh that moulded to the body's form.

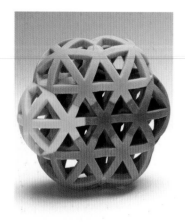

156
Z Corp
Colour 3D print sample

157
Z Corp
Adidas 3D prototype

158
Naoki Takizawa for Issey Miyake
Spring/Summer 2004

3D scanned body data will be essential information for the instant print, couture wardrobe. Various methods for scanning body-data exist, most of them requiring the customer to stand very still in a kiosk while lasers, cameras or radio waves capture their form from all angles. Once scanned, an image or 'point cloud' is created of the person, providing a mass of precise measurements. This information can then be used to tailor a garment.

In 2001, a 3D body-scanning group directed by Professor Philip Treleaven, based at the computer science department, University College London (UCL), conducted the UK National Sizing Survey. The project, known as Size UK, was sponsored by many major apparel retailers and scanned 11,000 people in a bid to gain accurate and up-to-date measurements of the UK consumer. The data from Size UK demonstrated a radical change in both men's and women's body shapes, which had become much bigger and more tubular since the last such survey was done in 1951. Similar findiings were revealed in subsequent surveys conducted in the US and Europe. Although this new data will enable retailers to offer a more accurate fit for the twenty-first century consumer, the demand for affordable made-to-measure clothing is rising. Traditionally, the made-to-measure wardrobe has consisted of businnesswear, but this is changing thanks to the new technology. BodyMetrics, a British 3D scanning company that has grown out of the UCL research, has a concession at Selfridges' flagship London store and is working with fashion designer Tristan Webber to produce designer jeans that customers can order made-to-measure. According to Suran Goonatilake, co-founder of BodyMetrics, the market is increasing for designer jeans priced at more than £100, with customers prepared to pay more for a good fit. Initially, the label 'Tristan Webber for Digital Couture' is offering two different styles.

159/160
At BodyMetrics's 3D scanning unit, a concession in Selfridges department store in London, a light scanner takes 200 measurements from each customer. Then, with the aid of 3D visualization software, the customer can see their measurements mapped onto different styles of jeans and can choose the ones they want. The specifications are sent to the factory where patterns are adjusted to create an individual fit. Two weeks' later a pair of designer jeans arrives with the customer's name and scan date embroidered on the garment label.

161/162
Tristan Webber showed his denim designs for Digital Couture as part of London Fashion Week in September 2004. His made-to-measure jeans were worn on the runway by supermodel Jodie Kidd whose famously long legs perfectly demonstrated the need for a tailored individual fit.

137

159
BodyMetrics
3D bodyscanning

160
BodyMetrics
Virtual try-on

161
Tristan Webber for Digital Couture
Spring/Summer 2005

162
Tristan Webber for Digital Couture
Spring/Summer 2005

Each client buying a pair of Digital Couture jeans will find their name and the date they were scanned embroidered on the inside: 'Jodie 09/04' replaces 'Waist 29, Leg 34' or a standard 8,10 or 12 size label.

This experiment offers a new retail model – no need for shops to buy-in stock. Instead, the store takes the form of a showroom, with sample collections from designers available for customers to inspect and select, but they order their own choice of size, colour and fabric. At present, it takes time for custom-made clothing to be ready – no good for that spontaneous purchase. But once a bodyscan can be fed straight into a 3D print machine the customer will be able to have immediate made-to-measure fashion. Goonatilake believes in-store production using 3D print will definitely happen and that 3D body-scanning technology will be a key enabler for this:

In twenty years' time I think it's possible you might have something equivalent to a scanner at home, a little unit that you might use for a whole bunch of things from taking your body-shape measurements to measuring bodyfat. Chances are this would replace your bathroom scales. You'll be able to replicate the in-store experience at home as well, but saying that, I think shopping will always remain a social experience.[3]

...fashion architects

Kyttanen and Delamore talk of building clothes and designing structures. Their vocabulary seems closer to that of an architect than a fashion designer. High fashion already has its share of architects turned fashion designers, and the future may see fashion designers looking to architectural processes to assist in the creation of

138

163/165
Paco Rabanne championed non-fashion materials such as lacquered aluminium discs and vinyl polychrome for his modernist designs. He was keen to challenge traditional methods of garment construction, preferring pliers and metal cutters to scissors and thread.

163
Paco Rabanne
Metal-link dress c.1965

164
Paco Rabanne
Metal-link mini dress, 1968

165
Paco Rabanne
Plastic evening dress, 1966

building dresses. The project Delamore and Kyttanen have embarked on is a long-term one. Delamore thinks that the ability to produce instant clothing using 3D print could be several years in the future: 2020. The seemingly simple idea of an 'instant' garment, creating a virtual shape and printing it out, will demand a highly complex mix of science and skills.

Even once the technology is developed, however, there is no guarantee that it will be embraced by other designers or consumers. Direct manufactured clothes are unlikely to replace more traditional forms of cloth or clothing production, especially where beauty lies in the evidence of the human hand. As Delamore states:

I don't think any of these 3D technologies will wipe anything out in one fell swoop. I can't envisage them being taken up wholesale – in 2020 people will still be practising 'shibori'[4] using thousand-year-old processes. 3D print will be just another layer of creative possibility. As with other fabric and fashion innovations, the first areas to embrace direct manufacturing will no doubt be military, medical and sport. As the wider potential is understood so it will filter down into the mainstream.[5]

Delamore also highlights the task of persuading designers to move into a virtual design environment. It is not yet known if the transition from manipulating fabric on the stand to doing the same in a virtual world is either feasible or desirable. Until *augmented reality* can be as sensitive to touch as real cloth, it is unlikely designers will migrate to this way of working. Any new technology will have to accommodate the spontaneity and experimental nature of creativity, and the flourish of inspiration. Visionaries like Delamore and Kyttanen are waiting for the technology to catch up with their creative ideas. As Delamore observes:

166
The K or multi-dress was the first do-it-yourself vinyl dress. The 250 interlocking pieces could clip together like a jigsaw in whatever shape the wearer chose. This modular kit offered a multitude of instant fashion possibilities.

167
This 1962 Instant Tweed Skirt was actually a sewing kit containing all the necessary articles to make a skirt – DIY fashion.

168
There have been many attempts to make vending machines for fashion but with limited success – women like to try things on or at least to see and feel a sample.

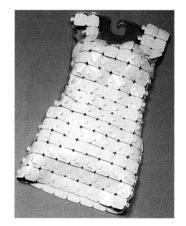

166
Pierre Bory
K dress, 1970

167
Instant Tweed Skirt, 1962

168
Bikini Automat, 1957

We've still got this problem of what people want to wear and why they want to wear it. I don't think engineers and chemists consider these things when it comes to commercialization. This is why so much technology ends up as a gimmick for a very short time instead of gradually seeping into the fabric of our lives.[6]

It is likely that people will always be attracted to traditional materials and the sensuousness of cloth against skin. Vending machines for clothing might be viable for acquiring wardrobe basics but they are unlikely to match the promise of luxury, leisure, indulgence and escape offered by the consumption of expensive fashion commodities. Long before luxury brands have to worry about instant 3D-printed fashion, they will have to contend with digital made-to-measure garments on the high street and in the shopping mall. If mass-market labels can start producing clothes that fit to perfection, what will happen to top-end designer fashion? It is unlikely that customers will continue to accept a 'standard' retail size, all of which vary from label to label, shop to shop and country to country.

Hi-tech mass-market clothing will compel high fashion to redefine itself. If fit is no longer the exclusive preserve of top-end designers, there will be increased emphasis on design, fabrication and finish. One day we may take our fashion fabricators for granted, regarding them with no more wonder than we do an inkjet printer. Garments manufactured from powder may result in clothes as we know them today, made using traditional materials and techniques, becoming a conscious style choice. Future trends may include a cult for cloth, a nostalgia for the stitch and a desire for exquisitely handcrafted embellishments.

169

Models are shown having couture toiles adjusted. The toiles in this image were made from Celanese (a man-made material of cellulose and acetate) which, when sprayed with a plasticizing acetate solution, shrank and stiffened into the desired shape, enabling the tailor to make further garments from the 'mould'.

170

The lined and interlined bra-section of this swimsuit is being treated with plastic adhesive and stretched over the sculpted form. This process now seems laborious compared with contemporary manufacture, such as 3D knitting.

169
Moulding suits, 1955

170
Bra sculpting, 1949

CHAPTER EIGHT /
THE
CARING
CAMISOLE

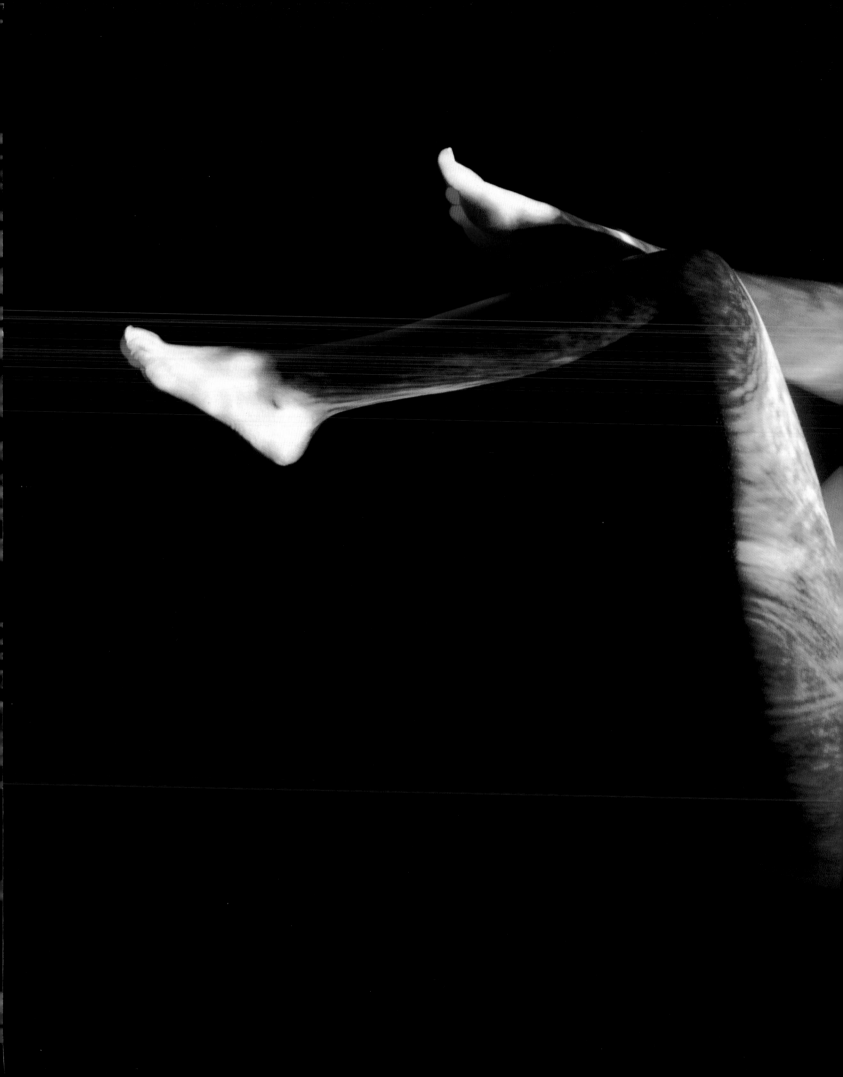

raymond
loewy
1939

It seems to me that the important improvements and innovations in clothes for the World of Tomorrow will be in the fabrics themselves. It is reasonable to assume that new types of fabrics will be developed which will greatly affect the design of clothes. Such fabrics, might, for, instance be constituted of microscopic cellular construction, made of a contracting and expanding fibre. When affected by atmospheric variations, the cells would automatically open or close and regulate air penetration. In other words, fabrics would be air-conditioned. Stitching will probably be replaced by some cementing or moulding process.

Protecting the human body from abrasion, extremes of temperature and weather is a fundamental function of clothing. Historically, technological innovation has largely been directed at specialized professional equipment for use by, for example, the military, firefighters, polar and space explorers or athletes. Research organizations are now offered incentives to find ways of transferring military and space technologies into everyday clothing that benefits a wider audience. A new generation of garment is envisaged that uses *e-textiles* and accommodates functions beyond the standard requirements of style, comfort and performance. In addition to providing protection from the elements, clothes are poised to take on a caring role, offering body-monitoring, drug treatment and even defence against physical attack or environmental accidents.

Our survival and well-being can be added to the list of functions we shall come to expect from protective clothing. A combination of factors is driving this technological research. In the West the demographic shift towards populations of older people is forcing a rethink of healthcare provision; clothing that can facilitate independent living might, for example, reduce the demand for residential care. Even the young and healthy are now taking a more active role in monitoring their lifestyle, and recording body performance has been used for some time in sport as an advantageous training tool. A climate of fear exists of terrorist attack as well as of less defined threats to the individual, and there is a perception that we are less safe than in the past. Responding to genuine concerns but arguably feeding the general paranoia, some researchers are investigating how clothing might warn or protect us from assault. Moves to address security for the average person may generate a market for personal protective wear. As never before, fabrics and clothing design are becoming a central focus for the improvement of daily life.

171
Major J.M. Adam, of the Medical Research Council, looks on as a wire vest and gloves for measuring mean skin temperature are demonstrated prior to an Antarctic expedition. In an emergency they could be heated from a battery or portable generator. They were hand-knitted by Major Adam's wife.

172
An early experiment in electrically heated clothing. Though progress has been made since then, the problem of powering a garment for any length of time has yet to be solved. Heavy portable batteries or even generators still have to be carried by the wearer and recharged at regular intervals.

149

171
Electrically heated clothes, 1957

172
Battery-heated coat, 1968

Keeping warm is critical to human survival. Until the late twentieth century we mostly relied on layers of clothes and fabric to protect us from the cold. Now, the basic need for insulating clothes is being met, more and more efficiently, by utilizing space technology. In 1999, Grado Zero Espace, the R&D department of the Italian brand Corpo Nove, developed Absolute Zero, a jacket that uses aerogel as a thermal liner. Aerogel, first discovered in the 1930s, is the best insulating material in the world, giving protection in temperatures as low as -50°C; it was used in 1997 to insulate space probes sent to Mars. In its purest form this material floats on air and NASA calls it 'frozen smoke'; it will make cold climate clothing as light as a feather.

For cold environments, where the body cools quickly and stays cold, heat-generating apparel is necessary and some outdoor clothing labels are now experimenting with electrically powered self-heating clothing. As early as 1917, during the First World War, pilots wore electrically heated silk flight suits, gloves and shoes. A temperamental and sometimes perilous garb, it was powered by generators often mounted externally on the aircraft. Powering electrically heated clothing is still challenging, with most garments able to heat up for only relatively short periods of time before the batteries need recharging. However, whereas older electrically heated clothing used metal wires that became hot, modern systems employ electro-conductive textiles. Gorix, a pioneer in this field, has developed a heated dive suit, powered by battery sticks mounted on the diver's air cylinders, for the marine equipment company Typhoon International. The heater pads placed in key anatomical areas are computer programmed to give the optimum heat output with safety and comfort. The North Face and Corpo Nove companies have also both used battery-powered heat pads slotted into outdoor gear.

150

173
Aerogel, manufactured at NASA's Jet Propulsion Lab, is a silicon-based solid with a porous, sponge-like structure, of which 99.8 per cent of the volume is air. Although ghostly in appearance, aerogel is hard to the touch. It is the best insulating material on earth.

174
This jacket was commissioned for the extreme climatic conditions of an Antarctic expedition. It was a development of Corpo Nove's earlier Absolute Zero garment and featured an outer membrane of Mitsubishi's Diaplex with an aerogel insulated lining.

175
Corpo Nove's Absolute Zero jacket contains powdered aerogel and keeps its wearer warm in temperatures as low as -50°C.

176
Based on a system used in US combat clothing during the Cold War, Corpo Nove's Cooling jacket needs 50 metres of 2-millimetre-wide plastic tubing for its internal cooling circuit.

177
Joseph Platt's 1939 imaginary design for American *Vogue* forecast fabrics that could be heated at will by the wearer. His electrically heated coat would be woven with fine wires to carry heat generated by batteries housed in the pockets.

173
NASA
Scientist Peter Tsou with aerogel

174
Corpo Nove
Absolute Frontier jacket, 2000

175
Corpo Nove
Absolute Zero jacket, 1999

176
Corpo Nove
Cooling jacket, 2000

177
Joseph Platt
Electrically heated coat, 1939

In 2000, Clothing+, the Finnish research centre of wearable technology, together with the clothing-manufacturer Reima, created a prototype snowsuit aptly called Cyberia.[1] More of a *smart* clothing system than a single garment, it went beyond providing electrically powered heat to offer the wearer an entire survival environment. A series of integrated garments with *sensors*, it could give information about the wearer's health, location and movements. In the event of an accident, either the wearer or the suit itself could transmit an SOS signal to a local emergency centre. The message would contain vital data regarding the person's physical state and geographical situation using a *Global Positioning System* (GPS). In addition to the electrical features, the suit included a special pocket for melting snow, waterproof pouches for matches, and ice spikes in the sleeves to help the wearer climb out of a hole.

As important as keeping warm is the ability to cool our bodies rapidly, allowing skin to breathe and perspire. The 1990s saw the emergence of fabrics intended to perform thermal regulation in a single layer. *Phase change materials* (PCMs) help regulate body temperature by absorbing and storing excess body heat so that it can be released back to the wearer as needed. The effect of PCMs is temporary and works best when the body is constantly undergoing fluctuations in temperature. PCMs remove and return heat but do not generate it.

...someone to watch over me

It used to be enough for a garment to keep us warm and dry, but with wearable technology and e-textiles clothes will be able to monitor our health, record vital data, administer treatment and even call for help. A nascent industry aims to provide individuals and organizations with smart diagnostic tools for remote monitoring of a person's well-being and health. Body-mounted devices and garments equipped with

178
The Typhoon XCM (eXtreme Climate Management) dive suit comprises a series of Gorix heater pads located in strategic anatomical areas. The pads are attached to the inner face of an undersuit constructed from materials with especially high insulation values. The power to heat the pads is derived from a slim stainless-steel battery stick mounted on the diver's air cylinders.

179
The heated jacket produced by the North Face, the outdoor clothing specialists, uses e-textile controls and interface so the wearer can regulate temperature. A battery system within the garment powers it for a few hours at a time.

180
This Finnish prototype smart clothing system was designed to assist survival in arctic conditions. It uses embroidered heart-rate sensors and Gorix heat pads, GSM communication – to send weather reports to the wearer or an automatic SOS message to base – and a Global Positioning System, as well as incorporating non-electrical features such as ice spikes.

181
A thermochromic film reveals the heated sections of an e-textile glove liner. The liner incorporates heating elements, thermal sensors and a power supply in a single woven component. It is powered by rechargeable batteries.

152

178
Gorix
Typhoon XCM dive suits, 2000

179
The North Face
Men's MET5 soft shell jacket, 2004

180
Reima Smart Clothing
Cyberia snowsuit, 2000

181
Intelligent Textiles
Heated glove liner, 2004

sensors can constantly check physiological signs: assisting athletes with training; patients with home recovery; or detecting symptoms when we are feeling unwell, warning us, a doctor or hospital, that medical aid is required.

A forerunner of future intelligent body-monitoring systems is the Sensatex SmartShirt, a T-shirt that combines advances in textile engineering, wearable computing and wireless data transfer. The SmartShirt was spun out of research conducted by a team led by Professor Sundaresan Jayaraman at Georgia Tech's School of Textile and Fiber Engineering. It was originally commissioned and funded by the Defense Advance Research Projects Agency (DARPA), the R&D arm of the US Department of Defense. Sensors attached to the body are then connected to the garment and measure *biometric* data: heart and respiration rate, body temperature and caloric burn. Readouts can be provided on a watch, PDA or by automated voice, and information can be wirelessly transmitted to a personal computer and thence to the Internet. The SmartShirt is an example of how military research — in this instance the goal of achieving an 'intelligent' combat garment — can also bring significant benefits to civilian life because it could be used for the chronically ill, the elderly and athletes. Body-monitoring is also being used for research into Sudden Infant Death Syndrome (SIDS). The Belgian company Verhaert, in conjunction with researchers at the University of Brussels, has developed the Mamagoose baby sleep suit that can be used by parents at home. It has integrated breathing and heart-rate sensors connected to a computer that monitors the sleeping infant and sounds an alarm at the first sign of an unusual reading.

Uses for body-monitoring currently focus on medical care, but in the long term the scope is likely to broaden, encouraging everyday use for personal lifestyle

182
The SmartShirt system incorporates advances in textile engineering, wearable computing and wireless data transfer in order to collect, transmit and analyse information about the wearer's personal health and lifestyle. It measures and/or monitors individual biometric data such as heart and respiration rate, body temperature and caloric burn, as well as lifestyle data. It provides readouts via a wristwatch, PDA or automated voice. Biometric information is wirelessly transmitted to a personal computer and, ultimately, the Internet.

183
The LifeShirt is currently being used in clinical trials and research. The data gathered during the wearer's daily routine provides pharmaceutical and academic researchers with a continuous 'movie' of the subject's health in everyday situations (work, school, exercise, sleep), rather than the 'snapshot' generated during a typical clinic visit. The LifeShirt system collects, analyses and reports on data about the subject's lung, heart and posture. It also compares data on blood pressure, skin temperature, respiration and other information collected by optional peripheral devices.

153

182
Sensatex
SmartShirt

183
VivoMetrics
LifeShirt

management. Ambient-care clothing might provide unobtrusive but detailed information on calorie intake and energy expended, while checking that all vital signs are normal. The collected information might provide useful insight to a specialist prescribing treatment or evidence for medical insurance. Caring undergarments might also administer daily drug doses, using a smart textile layer to effect the timed release of a substance through the skin.

...secret agents

The caring aspect of clothing may be applied on several levels. We already have anti-microbials within textiles that act invisibly to consume undesirable odours;[2] anti-UV fabrics, which help to shield us from the sun's harmful rays;[3] and silver encapsulated or coated anti-microbial fibres, which give protection from electro-magnetic radiation emitted by mobile phones and computers.[4] Investigations into bio-fabrics, as we have seen in Chapter 3, are also underway to produce self-cleaning fabrics containing bacteria that 'eat' dirt.

A collection of embedded functions in clothing may be activated only as and when needed. The terms 'context aware' and 'affective', describing the influence of user actions and emotions on how something operates,[5] are more familiar to computing or product design, but clothing is set to join this field as it starts to sense and respond to the wearer's environment or movements. Garments may house hidden protection, ready to spring into action in the event of an emergency, such as the ski jacket that inflates into a protective 'anti-avalanche' shelter worn by Pierce Brosnan in the 1999 James Bond film, *The World is Not Enough*. Inflatable lifejackets are an accepted essential at sea, and all modern vehicles have airbags installed, but it was only recently that companies began to integrate that technology into clothing. In 2001, the

184
The first generation of wearable body monitoring from BodyMedia has been in production for some years and takes the form of an armband module worn on the back of the upper right arm. A combination of sensors gathers data on movement, heat flux, skin temperature, near-body temperature and galvanic skin response. The HealthWear version collects low-level physiological and lifestyle data in order to determine the number of calories burned. It also contains two-way wireless communication capabilities so data can be uploaded direct to a computer.

185
The SenseWear patch is the next stage in wearable body monitoring – it can be applied to the wearer's skin like a simple band-aid. Instead of the wires and rigid cases associated with heart rate monitors, this small multi-sensor patch continuously collects, processes and stores more than 48 hours' worth of clinical heart rate and context-related data for presentation back to the wearer, a care provider or researcher.

186
From a design project of conceptual products for 2010, IDEO's future sports watches feature stopwatch, barometer and altimeter plus vital statistics and performance analysis conveyed wirelessly to a future PDA or 'Agent'. A hydro-gel adhesive back allows for comfortable wear, stretching with the user's skin, allowing moisture to pass through, and adhering for hours.

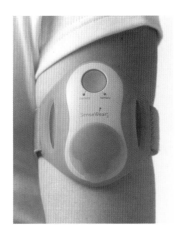

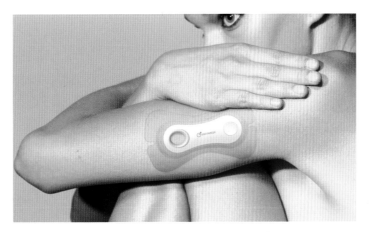

184
BodyMedia
SenseWear armband

185
BodyMedia
SenseWear patch

186
IDEO
Sports watch

Japanese manufacturer Mugen Denko started to sell Hit Air, a motorcycle jacket with a removable airbag system. The instant the rider is thrown from the bike the jacket inflates to form a tough cushion around the neck, vital organs and hips. A similar system may be of benefit to the elderly, who suffer frequent falls, distress from broken bones, and bruising that can take a long time to heal.

Portable personal alarms that provide reassurance, especially for women and senior citizens and their carers, have existed for some time. In the past these devices were worn around the neck or wrist, or in a pocket, and could be pressed to trigger a distress signal. In the future, clothing may incorporate alarm and GPS systems that can both call a designated person or emergency service and enable them to find the elderly person quickly. This function would be desirable for anyone at risk, whether medically or from external attack, such as the police and the military. There are also moves to use this technology to address the personal protection of vulnerable individuals, such as women at risk of domestic violence or who are being stalked.

An example of design for personal protection is the No-Contact Jacket, which delivers an electric shock to anyone attempting to grab its wearer. It was developed in 2002 specifically for women by Adam Whiton, an industrial designer at MIT, and Yolita Nugent, head designer at Advanced Research Apparel. The designers describe it as 'exo-electric armor' which, when activated by the wearer, pulses 80,000 volts of low amperage electric current just below the surface shell of the jacket. Whiton explains what happens when an assailant attacks the wearer:

The pain experienced is non-lethal but is enough of a shock to effectively and immediately deter contact with her body and provide a critical life-saving option for

187/188
An automatic airbag system for motorbike riders, the Hit Air jacket is attached via a fastener (similar to a seatbelt) to a coiled wire that is permanently secured to the bike frame. If the rider is thrown from the bike the coiled wire pulls a key out of a gas release mechanism and inert gas inflates the jacket in less than half a second, providing air cushion protection to the back, chest, neck and hips on impact. After a few seconds the jacket automatically starts to deflate and the air bags can be folded away for re-use.

187
Mugen Denko
Hit Air jacket, 2001

188
Mugen Denko
Hit Air jacket, air cushion fully inflated

escape. The goal of the No-Contact Jacket is to call attention to violence against women and to offer an alternative response to the body's vulnerable space and boundaries that society, culture and fashion have created.[6]

According to Whiton, the No-Contact Jacket was initially intended as a critical design project, aimed at raising more questions than it answers. The designers were surprised, therefore, when instead of people being outraged at the idea of wrapping women in a high-voltage electrified field, the feedback was positive – women found the garment not just acceptable but desirable. Some of them found the jacket more appealing than hand-held alarms, and even those who didn't feel particularly at risk thought it made an interesting political statement or symbol of empowerment. Whiton notes:

In the apparel industry I think consumers buy not out of 'need' but out of 'desire', specifically the desire to express who they are or wish to be. If technology can give apparel new abilities in which people can define and express themselves then certainly there will be a market for it. In our current day and age safety and security are very much desired and perhaps that is the appeal of the No-Contact Jacket for the many people we've heard from.[7]

It is intentionally provocative and does indeed raise concerns not usually associated with clothing. For example, in legal terms, might the wearer be sued for injuring an attacker? And if the jacket fell into the wrong hands could it be used as a weapon in its own right, possibly against the very person it was intended to protect? Whiton continues to explore these challenges and believes there is a place for clothing that assists us in meaningful ways:

189/192
The No-Contact Jacket is designed for women to use in situations where they feel threatened by physical attack. Before entering a potentially vulnerable area the wearer arms the system by means of a keyed lock. A LED indicator on the cuff then flashes red, announcing the system is armed. If threatened, the wearer can depress either of the two palm switches located in the cradle of each hand to discharge a high voltage electric current. When the switch is activated 80,000 volts of electricity pulses through conductive pathways just below the surface of the jacket. To warn off any potential unauthorized contact the jacket produces visible and audible electric arcs between two seams on the wearer's upper right shoulder. If an assailant grabs the wearer the shock and pain will disorientate them but not cause any lasting harm. The wearer is protected from the electric current by an insulated rubber layer built into the jacket. The No-Contact Jacket is designed specifically for women, who have more pronounced security concerns than men. Princess seams, fitted shape and narrow armholes are conscious design decisions to prevent men wearing what is meant to be a female garment. The jacket is intended for non-aggressive defence and is not meant to encourage violence.

157

189
Adam Whiton & Yolita Nugent
No-Contact Jacket – keyed lock

190
Adam Whiton & Yolita Nugent
No-Contact Jacket – activator

191
Adam Whiton & Yolita Nugent
No-Contact Jacket – electric arc

192
Adam Whiton & Yolita Nugent
No-Contact Jacket, 2002

I feel that if industry and academia pursue goals of apparel-embedded intelligence and contextually aware clothing the end result will have to do more than sense our feelings and play the appropriate MP3s. Our clothing will be in a prime position to respond to our most intimate problems and to a larger extent our most critical social agendas.[8]

...fear and loathing of clothing?

The future may point to people wearing a 'super shell' or 'sartorial architecture'. A single layer of clothing may simultaneously care, defend and attack. It might deliver medication, give protection from injury and fight pathogens. Today's somewhat awkward prototype body-monitoring garments and devices may lay the foundation for tomorrow's imperceptible caring camisole. A sleek biometric body-lining might be worn as a second skin or built into lingerie and underwear, and put on as part of our daily dressing ritual. In the same way that architecture accommodates invisible utilities, clothing might house the equivalent to heating and plumbing systems, ventilation, telecommunications, surveillance and so forth.

Researchers have even forecast garments that might 'sniff' the air, capable of detecting and detoxing chemical or biological agents.[9] At Siggraph's 2004 CyberFashion show, Paul Davies showed a Department of Homeland Security Safety Vest. His garment links wirelessly to the US Department of Homeland Security website, obtains the current threat status (a colour coding system) and downloads it to the vest, where it is electronically displayed.

Future clothing might not only warn or defend against attack but also act as evidence. Forensic fabrics or fashion might incorporate spy cameras and microphones to

193/194
Hussein Chalayan's 'Kinship Journeys' collection commented on religious themes and included ideas to do with resisting death. There were references to life-jackets and buoyancy throughout, symbolizing possible salvation, and culminating in a finale of garments that exploded into inflatable 'life' skirts.

193
Hussein Chalayan
Autumn/Winter 2003/4

194
Hussein Chalayan
Autumn/Winter 2003/4

capture an attacker's image or voice, and a special textile coating might collect fingerprints, hair or fibres. There is a danger, of course, that such clothing might engender a false sense of security, encouraging people to take risks that they wouldn't otherwise contemplate. Clothing intended to bring comfort and freedom may in fact heighten paranoia and invade privacy.

If clothing becomes a hub of personal data, this information will have value to outside agencies. We may be heading for a time when insurance companies demand access to an individual's communicating wardrobe. Would we be happy to comply with this request if it meant we paid a lower premium? Garments equipped with personal-data capture will give rise to concerns never before encountered in dress. Fashion and clothing may become a highly political arena and part of a wider debate on personal privacy, human rights and public security.

195
Before the Second World War, bullet-proof vests had metal plates inserted into a cotton garment. In 1965, DuPont lightened body armour with the creation of Kevlar – an aramid fibre five times stronger than steel on an equal-weight basis. However, we are still a long way from a single, unobtrusive protective fabric layer for use in everyday clothing.

196
Attempts to address assault in the street have yielded mixed results over the decades. In 1961, inventor John Walter Fisher demonstrated his design of a special 'security' bag and hat. When stolen, the bag sounded a whistle and three extending arms clamped the hand attempting to open it. The fibreglass bowler hat could withstand the blows of the assailant's cosh.

197
Referencing Edvard Munch's painting The Scream, CP Company designed a jacket for urban protection that released a cry to scare off an attacker and to alert nearby help. The Munch jacket housed a personal safety device inserted into a special pocket, activated by a pull-cord if the wearer was assaulted.

198
Karrysafe products are designed to combat the four most common means of bag theft: dipping, grabbing, lifting, slashing. Bags feature slash-proof materials, combination locks and an alarm that will automatically start screaming if the bag is snatched.

195
Bullet-proof vests, c.1938

196
Accessories for protection against street assault, 1961

197
CP Company
Munch jacket, 1998

198
Vexed Generation
Karrysafe bag, 2002

THE
TALKING
T-SHIRT

sonia
delaunay
1935

I imagine the future of fashion in these terms: there will be design centers, research laboratories that will deal with practical applications, constantly adapting to the changing conditions of life. Research into the materials used and a simplification of aesthetic notions will become increasingly important. On such carefully considered and up-to-date foundations, vision and sensuality will find a wide field opening up before them.

199
Radio hat, 1922

We are familiar with clothing conveying visual meanings about who we are, but what of its involvement with the other four senses – touch, hearing, smell and even taste? Newly emergent technologies, such as *radio-frequency identification* (RFID), *Bluetooth wireless networking*, *Global Positioning Systems* (GPS), *sensors*, *actuators* and woven radio antennae will soon let smart clothing do the talking for us. *E-textiles* will equip the wearer with a new level of communication at work, in the home and socially. A techno-fashion vocabulary is emerging that is expressive and emotive. Fashion could react to *biometric* data gathered from the wearer's body, such as heart rate or pheromone emission, or external signals received from someone or something else. Body-responsive garments will emit light, perfume or sound, and change colour or vibrate. Clothes in the future wardrobe will be able to talk to each other, to people around us, to machines, architecture and even satellites.

So far, RFID has been used in clothing to track a product through the supply chain from the factory via the retail outlet to the customer. It is now becoming clear, however, that there are far more creative possibilities for this technology. For example, conveniently located electronic readers on doors might scan for certain products, presenting brands with unique marketing and promotional opportunities. Fashion houses might embed chips in their products so that, for instance, limited edition shoes or a bag might admit you to the VIP area of a club, become a backstage pass at a concert or fashion show, or offer upgrades at the airport.

...wearing your heart on your sleeve

E-textiles will enable fabrics and fashion to speak more eloquently than ever before. Nothing will be left to chance – we may be able to send overt signals of availability or attraction to potential partners. Clothing might suddenly light up or glow a different

199
An early portable radio (or wireless) built into a hat and attached to headphones.

200
Artist Benoît Maubrey and Die Audio Gruppe make wearable sonic art: clothing augmented with electronic components that is worn to perform and create public sound environments. Early experiments started with Audio Jackets, second-hand clothing onto which loudspeakers were sewn. These first prototypes were equipped with portable cassette players and 10-watt amplifiers and played pre-recorded cassettes. In this image, H.J. Tauchert wears an electroacoustic jacket, cassette player, and amplifier (30 watts, 12 volt).

201
The electronic skirt of Maubrey's Audio Ballerina is based on a tutu. The Plexiglas surface is equipped with digital memories, looping devices (mini 257K samplers), radio-wave receivers, microphones, light sensors, amplifiers and speakers that enable the Audio Ballerina to interact directly with the environment by recording, producing and mixing live sounds. The tutu is powered either by solar cells or rechargeable batteries, depending on if it is an indoor or outdoor performance. The solar-powered electroacoustic tutu shown here is a performance costume with digital sampler, photoresistors, amplifier, pre-amplifier and radio receiver (30 watts, 12 volt). Audio Ballerinas are able to create an entire spectrum of sounds via their clothing.

167

200
Benoît Maubrey
Audio Jacket, 1983

201
Benoît Maubrey
Audio Ballerina, 1989

colour, a dress might blush for us, release a 'come hither' scent, emit a meaningful sound, or simply send a verbal message or phone number. Actuating fabrics will mean a garment can stroke someone's arm without you touching them, should you so desire.[1]

Emotionally expressive clothes may help those searching for love or friendship to find a partner. Since the late 1990s, Japanese teenagers have been seduced by the Lovegety bleeper, a wearable electronic device that the owner can set to the kind of activitiy he or she is interested in: talk, karaoke or 'get2' (meaning anything goes). When the badges come within fifteen feet of each other and are in the same mode, they bleep and the 'get' light flashes to alert the potential lovebirds. France Télécom has gone one step further: instead of a badge that issues a sound, they have created a wireless wearable display embedded in a garment, which can flash images or a message straight to a suitor. The French fashion designer Elisabeth de Senneville worked with the company's researchers to produce a range of clothing called CreateWear, which incorporates the removable flexible screens. The wearer can generate animations, patterns or messages on a mobile phone and send them to the electronic display using a *multimedia messaging service* (MMS). A potential icebreaker in awkward situations, a 'talking' T-shirt would enable people to conduct tentative visual communications before plucking up the courage to speak. It might, for example, help someone to indicate their interest in a stranger sitting opposite them on a train. This ties in with the views of Emeric Mourot, R&D project manager at France Télécom:

Clothes are becoming a key interface for giving graphic expression and form to your moods. It's a very personal symbolism, an emotion or state of mind that you can

202
Joanna Berzowska's Memory Rich Clothing aims to sense and display traces of memory on clothes. These garments record acts of intimacy and indicate the time that has elapsed since the events have occurred. The Intimate Memory shirt has a sensitive microphone in the collar and a series of light points in a flower pattern on its front. When a friend or partner whispers something in your ear, the microphone records it and the lights glow. The number of lights indicates the intensity of the event. Over time, the lights turn off, one by one, to show how long it has been since the intimate event took place. The skirt has touch sensors incorporated into it. In the course of the day, the skirt records each touch event, and gradually starts changing colour to show how often it has come into contact with people or objects.

203
Jenny Tillotson is researching 'the living dress as a sensitive Smart Second Skin'. The dress mimics the body's circulation system, senses and scent glands. Aromatic messages are electronically 'pulsed' through wires to key points in order to activate the smell centre that emits a selection of scents, depending on your mood.

204
As part of Philips' New Nomads project, body piercing was given a technological slant with designs for piercings that glow and pulsate when the wearer is paged.

202
Joanna Berzowska
Intimate Memory, 2004

203
Adeline Andre & Jenny Tillotson
Smart Second Skin dress, 2002

204
Philips
New Nomads – glowing piercings, 2000

now display publicly and very simply through eye-catching animated graphics and short texts.[2]

CreateWear prototypes consist of a colour screen and a rechargeable battery that need to be removed before washing but can be transferred to other clothes or bags. The electronic components have been soldered to a flexible circuit board packaged in a fabric-layered sandwich. France Télécom plans to begin commercial production in the near future. Ultimately, the entire garment might become a fabric display.[3] The crudeness and gimmicky nature of these attempts to create clothing that communicates inner feelings is likely to appeal initially to teenagers who have grown up with text messaging and technologically mediated relationships. But for many single adults, a clothing system that performs the same function, albeit in a more sophisticated fashion, would be attractive. And as France Télécom also realizes:

Possible applications exist in the professional event marketing and communications sectors (the staff coordinating events could display real-time information for the visitors) or in advertising, public safety, etc.[4]

...musical mode

In the spring of 1939 the Italian couturier Elsa Schiaparelli showed a collection of music-themed garments that were accessorized with hats, bags and belts concealing tinkling music boxes.[5] Forty years later, in 1979, Sony launched its Walkman, the first portable personal cassette player, urging people to 'Put pride in your stride, a dip in your hip, the beat in your feet.' In the summer of 2000 Levi's and Philips Electronics launched the first commercial fashion collection to combine electronics with music and mobile communication.

205/208

France Télécom worked with French fashion designer Elisabeth de Senneville on a range of 'Wearable Communication' prototype garments. A flexible colour screen is incorporated into clothes and accessories to provide visual communication using mobile services. The screen is wirelessly connected to a mobile phone via Bluetooth technology, this in turn communicates with a remote server or with other people's terminals through GPRS and MMS. Images, animations and messages can be updated as often as the wearer chooses.

170

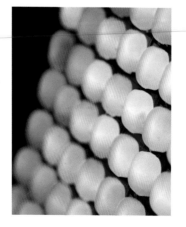

205
France Télécom
CreateWear, 2004 – components

206
France Télécom
CreateWear – active displays

207
France Télécom
CreateWear – display close-up

208
France Télécom
CreateWear – mobile programming

The resulting line, designed by Massimo Osti of CP Company, was called ICD+ (Industrial Clothing Design+) and featured jackets equipped with a Philips mobile phone and MP3 player, with a microphone integrated into the collar and storage for the earphones. A *personal area network* (PAN) linked the devices to a unified remote control, allowing the wearer, for example, to mute the music in order to take an incoming phone call. ICD+ was intended to appeal to 'urban nomads' – contemporary, techno-savvy, roving city dwellers who could afford the £800 price tag. Although the jacket itself was not electronic, it merely housed the technology which had to be removed when the garment was washed, ICD+ was an important landmark in the development of wearable electronics. Philips and Levi's experienced many technical and manufacturing difficulties in realizing the project, but nonetheless Philips was inundated with enquiries from fashion labels, keen to learn about the potential uses of electronics within apparel. Philips continues to work on wearable electronics but recognizes that the technology needs to become integral to the garment – to 'disappear into it'. Paul Gough, former head of Wearable Technologies at Philips Research Laboratories at Redhill in the UK, believes we have moved on some way from ICD+:

We now have things like fabric wiring. Although not very exciting, at the time, with the Levi's jacket, we still didn't have that as a reliable option. At this instant I can imagine using fabric wiring, fabric antennas – there is a collection of 'soft' electrical components that can be used nowadays. I think we're at an exciting point where we'll start to see a lot more experimentation.[6]

Since Philips and Levi's pioneering venture into wearable electronics, there have been other commercial fashion–electronic link-ups. Snowboarding brands are starting to

209/210
The ICD+ range was the result of the first commercial collaboration between a fashion brand, Levi's, with an electronics company, Philips. The intention of the project was to bring workwear up to date for the modern urbanite, designing clothing that would equip the wearer with the latest in mobile technology. The ICD+ line featured four jackets, each with a built-in Philips Xenium GSM phone, Philips Rush MP3 player, earphones, remote control and microphone. Wires concealed in the garment connected the fully integrated communications system. The microphone, inserted in the jacket collar, included voice-dialing capabilities, enabling the wearer to hear both music and phone calls through the earphones. To make a call the wearer flipped up the collar; MP3s were accessed in a pocket and buttons on the sleeve adjusted volume controls. The jackets were produced in limited numbers for premium retailers in the European market and although they sold well for two seasons the project was eventually terminated. ICD+ was a pioneering project that generated immense excitement and opened the doors to subsequent developments in fashion and wearable electronics.

209
Philips-Levi's
ICD+ Mooring jacket, 2000

210
Philips-Levi's
ICD+ Mooring jacket, 2000

use 'soft' interfaces to music in their clothing in the form of keypads on sleeves that operate pocketed MP3 players. Tactile fabric keypads and controls are being made by companies such as Softswitch, Eleksen and Gorix in the UK. They are a new genre of manufacturer making e-textile sensing and switching fabrics that can detect pressure and recognize when, where and how they are touched. These intuitive fabric controls are truly part of the garment: no hard components or wires, just soft, flexible and washable control.

Prior to the e-textiles era, the familiar sounds emitted by clothing were the rustle of silk taffeta, the crunch of cotton, or the creak of leather. The sound that clothes make when moving with the body is an important part of their erotic charge. But in addition to the traditional aural sensuality of fabrics, e-clothing may in due course become musical. Researchers at Virginia Tech in the US have already created fabric that can 'listen',[7] so what if it might also generate sound? Despina Papadopoulos's shoes, ClickSneaks, contain in each sole a sensor, sound chip, speaker and amplifier that make her sneakers sound like clicking stilettos. She walks down the street in comfort but sounds glamorous. Might future clothing talk to us or imitate other garments, objects or animals? A tie that whispers breathing or relaxation exercises before a public speech? Woolly mittens that chat like a child's favourite cartoon character? Or a leopard-print overcoat that purrs like a cat? Could we overhear fashionistas trying to identify a particular garment saying, 'It sounds like Christian Dior'?

...pleisurewear

Transmitting the sense of touch sounds like something taken straight out of a science-fiction novel. Whereas the sensing fabrics discussed above can detect pressure, actuating fabrics might apply pressure. Chapter 6 explored *electroactive polymers*

211
Softswitch, a division of Canesis Network Ltd, has been a pioneer in developing soft, fabric interfaces to wearable electronics, like this keypad.

212
In January 2003, Burton Snowboards and Apple unveiled the Burton Amp, the world's first wearable electronic jacket with an integrated iPod control system. Softswitch technology allows the iPod stored in a chest pocket to be controlled through a soft textile control pad integrated in the arm of the jacket. Snowboarders simply touch the control pad on the jacket sleeve to change songs or volume levels.

213
Conductive fabric tracks are woven into the O'Neill Hub snowboarding jacket and connect an Infineon Technologies' chip module to an Eleksen fabric keyboard and to built-in speakers/headset in the helmet. The chip module contains an MP3 player and a Bluetooth module via which the snowboarder can control a mobile phone. A microphone is in the collar.

214
For the ClickSneaks, the 'click' sound of high heels is recorded on a voice chip, while a speaker, amplifier and a sensor acting as a 'switch' on the sole of each foot transform these seemingly normal sneakers into a flighty performance. Part fantasy, part irony, the ClickSneaks subvert the traditional attributes of a pair of shoes.

173

211
Softswitch
Fabric keypad on sleeve

212
Burton
Amp snowboarding jacket, 2003

213
O'Neill
Hub snowboarding jacket, 2004

214
5050
ClickSneaks, 2004

(EAPs) made into fibres that can be activated to change shape with the application of an electric current. A fabric made from EAP fibres could be made to tense or relax by turning current on and off, and when combined with a woven antenna that picks up a mobile phone signal, someone could dial up a person's garment and activate the fabric to give a remote hug.

Actuating fabrics presage a whole new form of clothing that is electronically tactile. Specific areas of clothing could be targeted, creating effects that give the wearer a sense of shivers running down their spine or of a creature running up their arm. A parent might be able to give a child a remote 'squeeze' of the hand. The action of stroking one's own sleeve could send that sensation to a partner, friend or relative. To say that one has been 'touched' by someone or something may no longer be a simple turn of phrase. Remote communication of human touch could convey closeness, comfort and security. But expressions of emotion could also be used to negative effect – a highly tuned garment might bruise or shock its wearer. This might find an application in gaming. At present, players of computer games can experience punches or blows felt through force feedback on a joystick, the result of *haptic* design. Tactile gaming might take this form of physical interaction to a new level; players could don suits that allow them to subject their whole body to a game environment.

Tactile clothing could offer the wearer a real physical experience of any number of situations, whether at the movies, in a computer game, at a theme park or adult entertainment. It might find its uses in skills improvement for sport tuition, for example in indicating to a tennis player how to correct a stroke, or helping a footballer keep contact with the ball. Therapeutic clothing might massage office workers at their desks or help deliver physiotherapy to a patient. 'Pleasurewear' might consist of a total-body

215
Stead's garments are intended to 'live' around the house. They suggest that clothing which is unworn could assume a new emotive function by reacting to human presence. *In situ*, a proximity sensor detects when someone comes near, triggering a 'response' from the garment. Icarus, a delicate feathered shrug, has four (Gorix) heat panels sandwiched between the feathers and the lining which become warm when activated, heating up the feathers that are coloured with thermo-chromic dyes so they change from blue to green.

216
PikMe is a scarf that craves the comfort of human touch and the warmth of a neck. PikMe uses three colours of electroluminescent (EL) wire woven within a tactile knit and a proximity sensor to activate a response. Emotive colours intimate self-harm, and the EL wire is used to illuminate blue 'veins', turquoise 'bruises' and red 'gashes'.

217
Desirée uses electroluminescent 'sequins' encased in velvet that light up to 'flirt' with the viewer. She is sexy and provocative – when she senses your presence she shimmers, her signals becoming more excited as you draw nearer, imitating the human gaze. Desirée's EL panels are dyed in deep hues to alter the colour of the light as it glows from within the garment – her sequins illuminate in a pattern that increasingly courts your attention.

215
Lisa Stead
Icarus, 2004

216
Lisa Stead
PikMe, 2004

217
Lisa Stead
Desirée, 2004

sensor suit, something sought after in the field of *teledildonics*, a computer-mediated sexual interaction between distant people, where sensations are transmitted from one partner to another.

...dressing up and staying in

Talking T-shirts may not really speak out loud – what an anti-social, noisy annoyance that would be. But it does seem probable that clothes are about to start communicating in new, more intricate ways. An approach to the design of electronic products is emerging that seeks to 'soften' technology. As electronics become textile- and clothing-based, they will be integrated into a familiar, tactile, human-centred world. The convergence of fashion and electronics necessitates collaboration between engineers and textile and fashion designers.

The role of dress as a rich communicator central to all our interactions in life can potentially be reinforced by adding variations of the sensations of touch, hearing, smell and maybe even taste to what we wear. Clothing that can provoke, respond to and record physical and emotional experiences will perhaps encourage new social connections, intimacy, and shared interests and memories. Evocative, expressive and emotional dress may promote and increase the possibility of chance encounters.

Any new technology inevitably raises concerns. In tailoring technology to the individual, new scenarios are created that could pose a threat to the wearer's personal security, privacy and freedom. If intimate details of identity are housed in what we wear, our clothing may be at increased risk of electronic eavesdropping, theft and fraud. These are some of the challenges that will face designers of communicating clothes.

218
A collaboration between Studio 5050 and the New York-based fashion collective As Four, the Courtly bags take the form of As Four's signature circular bag. Infrared receivers, transmitter and a PIC chip (programmable interrupt controller) control embedded LEDs and speakers. When a bag detects a 'mate' it lights up and emits a chirping sound. They start timidly only to envelope the wearer in a storm of light and staccato electronic twittering. Courtly bags refer back to the medieval concept of courtly love – sophisticated flirtations that went on for months. A frisson occurs between wearers of the theatrical bags – a sort of dance of manners.

219/220
The HugJackets demand a deliberate act of physical union. An embrace between the two wearers activates a pattern of LEDs and a 'bombastic' sound. An intricate quilted pattern made of conductive fabric is sewn on the front of each jacket. When two people wearing a HugJacket embrace they power each other up through that pattern. The energy transfer is both symbolic and actual and the embrace is instantly translated into an explosion of light and sound. The HugJackets' technology is simple; it is the intricate patterning and placement of the conductive fabric that allows for the surprising connection and effect to take place. The two jackets, through their twinned pattern, literally plug into each other's battery source.

175

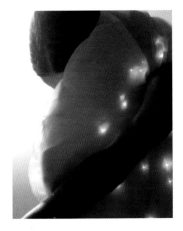

218
5050/As Four
Courtly bags, 2002

219
5050
HugJackets, 2004

220
5050
HugJackets, 2004

Wireless connectivity and always-on networks mean we will have constant access to the outside world, but likewise, unless we choose to opt out, it will have constant access to us. The proliferation of talking T-shirts will mean we are connected even when remote from people, with garments becoming portals between us and our environment.

At present we don particular styles of clothing for leisure or pleasure pursuits but in the future we may see the arrival of 'questwear' – garments that help us to seek information, support or love. E-textiles and the new functionality they might bring to fashion may result in the garment becoming a medium and an activity in its own right.

221/222
Cute Circuit's KineticDress reacts to the wearer's walking pace and activity (talking, moving, shaking hands, etc.) and adapts to it. The dress has sensors, actuators, and a microprocessor with a special algorithm able to read the sensor patterns. The algorithm calibrates the first time the dress is worn and 'understands' when the user walks fast or slow, changing the light patterns on the skirt accordingly. When still, the dress is dark.

223
Fashion Victims is a critical design project conceived and developed at the Interaction Design Institute, Ivrea, Italy, by Davide Agnelli, Dario Buzzini and Tal Drori. It uses clothing as the medium for making the invisible world of electronic radiation visible. As more and more phone calls are conducted in the bag wearer's surroundings, it leaks coloured ink. Once the bag has reached a point where the owner does not want it to be stained anymore, the mechanism can be pulled out and the bag used normally.

224
A future concept for 2010, using low-power, nano-derived technology, GPS Toes are toe rings that would link with a GPS receiver kept in a purse or worn on a belt. Wearing one on each foot, the wearer would be guided to a pre-set destination by vibrations and a light that signals direction changes. The left toe ring would indicate left turns and the right toe right turns.

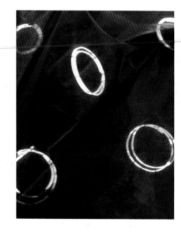
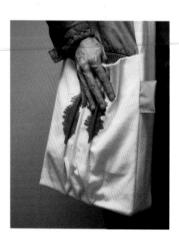
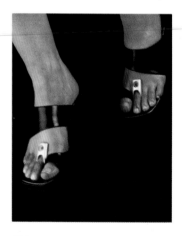

221
Cute Circuit
KineticDress, 2004

222
Cute Circuit
Detail of KineticDress, 2004

223
Fashion Victims
Bag, 2003

224
IDEO
TechnoJewelry – GPS Toes

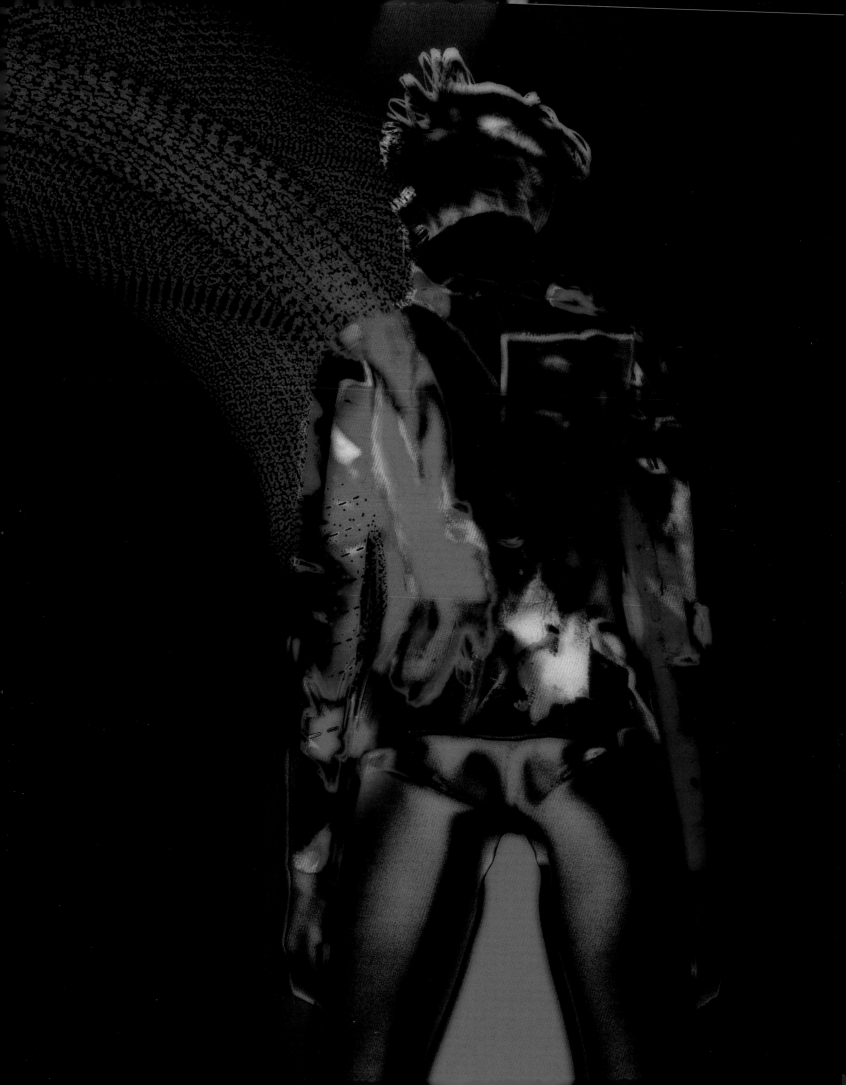

THE
SELF-ASSEMBLING
RAINCOAT

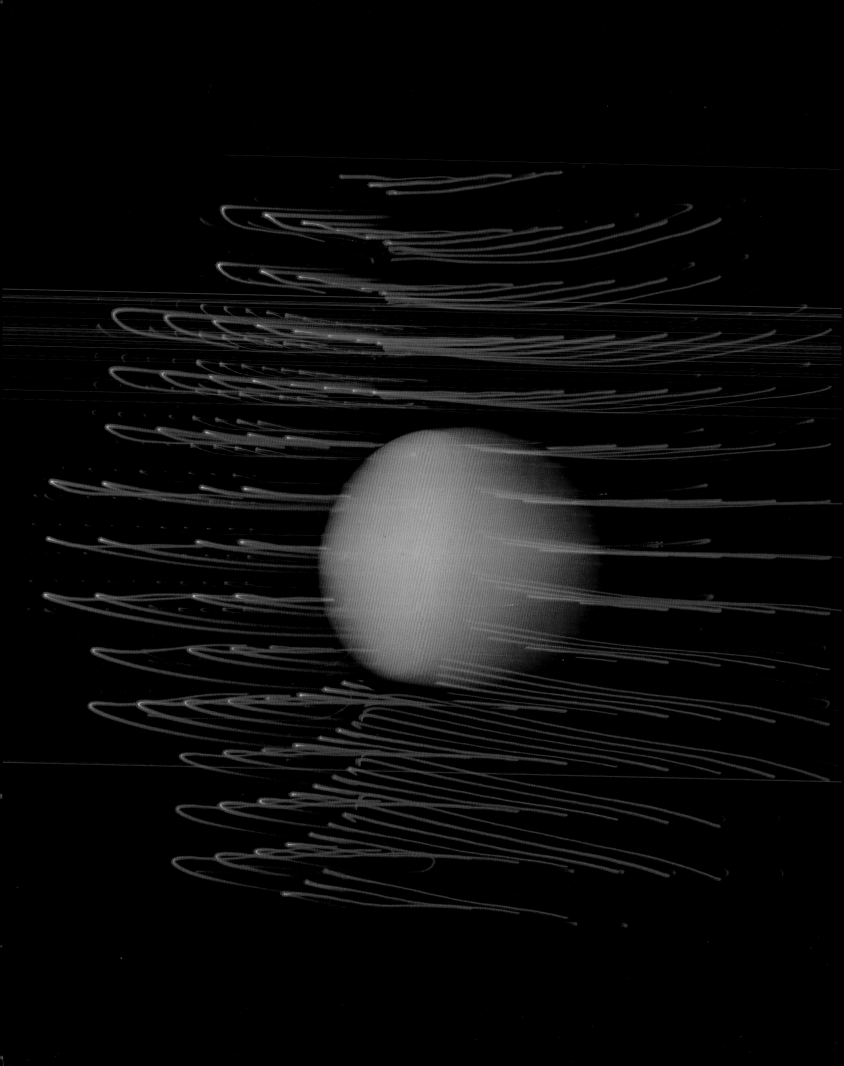

neal stephenson 1995

The veil was a field of microscopic, umbrella-like aerostats programmed to fly in a sheet formation a few inches in front of Nell's face. The umbrellas were all pointed away from her. Normally they were furled, which made them nearly invisible; they looked like the merest shadow before her face, though viewed sideways they created a subtle wall of shimmer in the air. At a command from Nell they would open to some degree. When fully open, they nearly touched each other. The outside-facing surfaces were reflective, the inner ones matte black, so Nell could see out as if she were looking through a piece of smoked glass. But others saw only the shimmering veil. The umbrellas could be programmed to dangle in different ways – always maintaining the same collective shape, like a fencing mask, or rippling like a sheet of fine silk, depending on the current mode.

In his 1995 cult science-fiction novel, *The Diamond Age*, Neal Stephenson describes a future where fashion fabrics made from 'fabricules' are 'thinner than soap bubbles';[1] 'matter compilers', installed in people's houses, create goods to order, assembling individual molecules that are sent down a pipe known as a 'Feed'; and elite designers, who write programmes that organize atoms, create intricate products from their offices housed in a place known as 'Bespoke'. Not for the first time, science fiction and fact are overlapping. In Stephenson's strangely familiar neo-Victorian world (the novel is set in the reign of Queen Victoria II), engineers labour under a fresco of Richard Feynman, Ralph Merkle and Eric Drexler – a nod to three celebrated contemporary scientists who have made significant contributions to the field of *nanotechnology*.

In 1959, the physicist Richard Feynman gave a talk at the California Institute of Technology (Caltech) entitled 'There's Plenty of Room at the Bottom'. In this now famous presentation, he outlined his vision of rearranging atoms, the very building blocks of our world. He noted, 'When we get to the very, very small world – say circuits of seven atoms – we have a lot of new things that would happen that represent completely new opportunities for design.'[2] Feynman hypothesized that the ability to manipulate matter on an atomic scale would enable us to make materials with entirely different properties, using completely new methods of manufacture. Instead of relying on structures designed by nature, we could design and build our own. When Feynman talked of a 'very, very small world', he was referring to the nanoscale and below. The prefix 'nano' comes from the Greek meaning 'dwarf' – a nanometre is one thousand-millionth of a metre. To help put this in perspective, 'one nanometre is to a human hair as a human hair is to the thickest redwood tree',[3] or how much your fingernails grow each second.

225/226
When film director Richard Fleischer visualized nanotechnology for the movie-going public in 1966, it was still very much an unfamiliar science-fiction concept. In *Fantastic Voyage*, based on Isaac Asimov's novel, a surgical team and their submarine are miniaturized and inserted into the bloodstream of a dying man to destroy a life-threatening blood clot deep in his brain. The microscopic submarine *Proteus* and its occupants are faced with a perilous journey threatened by collisions with white blood cells and attack from antibodies. *Fantastic Voyage* helps to illustrate the exceptionally small scale referred to in nanotechnology. The real science of contemporary nanomedicine and nanorobots imagines a future where molecular-scale machines will indeed be implanted into the human body to operate medical procedures. Robert Freitas in his book *Nanomedicine* claims 'Nanomedicine will eliminate virtually all common diseases of the 20th century, virtually all medical pain and suffering, and allow the extension of human capabilities – most especially our mental abilities.'

225
Fantastic Voyage, 1966

226
Fantastic Voyage, 1966

The field of nanotechnologies encompasses biology, physics, chemistry, computer science and materials engineering.[4] Nanotechnology is not strictly a new discipline – scientists were indirectly manipulating molecules for most of the twentieth century. In 1934 a DuPont chemist, Dr Wallace Carothers, discovered a chemical reaction that strung molecules together to form a *polymer* fibre – this was 'nylon', the world's first synthetic silk.

...the nano-wardrobe

Clothing fabrics have often been the first beneficiaries of new developments in science and technology. The textile industry was at the forefront of innovation in the Industrial Revolution and is leading the way in the commercialization of nanotechnology. In the short term, fashion consumers are likely to encounter nanotechnology in the form of special textile finishes pioneered by companies such as Nano-Tex and Schoeller. These fabrics look and feel like any other, but repel stains, resist wrinkles and fight bacteria. Since they require less frequent washing and can be laundered at lower temperatures than traditional cloth, today's nano-surfaced fabrics are also more environmentally friendly. In the very long term, we might all create our own nanotech fashion that will not need any washing at all.

In their 1991 book, *Unbounding the Future*, Eric Drexler, Chris Peterson and Gayle Pergamit forecast truly *smart* cloth:

With nanotechnology, even the finest textile fibers could have sensors, computers, and motors in their core at little extra cost. Fabrics could include sensors able to detect light, heat, pressure, moisture, stress, and wear, networks of simple computers to integrate this data, and motors and other nanomechanisms to respond to it.

227
Nano-Tex has developed a family of fabric treatments with nanoscale molecules that attach to fibres and provide optimal performance. Nano-Tex finishes repel liquids, resist stains, stay drier and release 'ground in' stains. They are developed on a nanoscale – one million times smaller than a grain of sand – so fabric remains breathable and maintains its performance and desirable feel through the life of the garment. The image shows a 100 per cent silk tie from Brooks Brothers with a Nano-Tex 'resists spills' finish that means red wine cannot penetrate the surface.

228
Schoeller's NanoSphere mimics self-cleaning surfaces found in nature such as the lotus leaf, whose microscopic rough surface structure prevents dirt from adhering. Like Nano-Tex, Nano-Sphere is a finishing technology that improves the performance of traditional textile fibres. Schoeller promotes NanoSphere as an environmentally friendly product as it means fabrics require less frequent washing and can be laundered at lower temperatures.

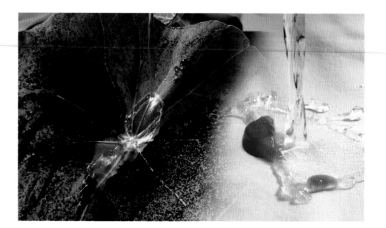

227
Nano-Tex
Nano-Tex finish

228
Schoeller
NanoSphere finish

Ordinary, everyday things like fabric and padding could be made responsive to a person's needs – changing shape, color, texture, fit, and so forth – with the weather and a person's posture or situation. This process could be slow, or it could be fast enough to respond to a gesture. One result would be genuine one-size-fits-all clothing (give or take child sizes), perfectly tailored off the rack, warm in winter, cool and dry in summer; in short, nanotechnology could provide what advertisers have only promised.[5]

...fashioning molecules

Nanotechnological processes can manufacture products in two ways: 'top-down', re-forming bulk material into something smaller; and 'bottom-up', assembling tiny bits to make bigger structures. The former has resulted in the nano-surface textures now appearing in clothing. The latter, potentially more exciting but still only just nascent, is referred to as *molecular manufacturing* or *molecular nanotechnology*. In this method, atoms can be individually positioned or, ultimately, made to self-assemble. This area of science imagines universal assemblers able to build structures, molecule by molecule, according to a set of instructions – just like the engineers and programmers in Stephenson's *Diamond Age*. Fabrics and fashion could be designed from the molecule up, allowing for all manner of new aesthetic and functional possibilities.

The Institute for Molecular Manufacturing (IMM), a non-profit foundation in Los Altos, California, conducts and supports research in this field, and predicts:

During the early decades of the twenty-first century, the advent of practical molecular manufacturing technology will make it possible to fabricate inexpensively almost any structure allowed by the laws of physics. Consequences will include immensely

229

A key breakthrough in nanotechnology came in 1985 when Robert F. Curl, Sir Harold Kroto and Richard Smalley discovered a third form of pure carbon molecule, the other two being graphite and diamond. They named it 'Buckminsterfullerene', after visionary architect R. Buckminster Fuller's famous geodesic dome for the 1967 Montreal Expo. The new molecule was made up of sixty carbon atoms arranged like a soccer ball, and it has since become known as a buckyball or fullerene. The spherical shape of buckyballs makes them very stable and they are capable of withstanding high temperatures and pressures. Because they are hollow they can be filled with other molecules so they might, for example, deliver a drug to a specific type of cell in the human body. So far, they have led to the study of carbon nanotubes (CNTs).

230

Carbon nanotubes are also known as buckytubes. Experiments suggest that they are incredibly tough. Other properties – such as electrical conductivity – seem to vary with the particular geometry of the tube. This means it could be possible to have two concentric nanotubes, one inside the other, the outer one acting as an insulator and the inner one conducting a current. Contemporary research is attempting to make or spin the nanoscale tubes into a useable fibre. Once achieved, this technology could be exploited to add new functionality for fashion and textiles.

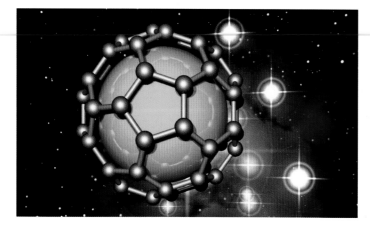

229
Chris Ewels
Buckyball

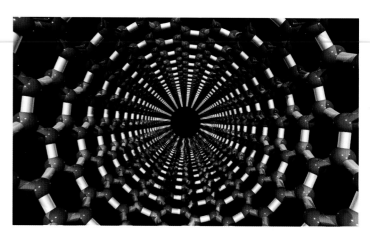

230
Chris Ewels
Carbon nanotube

powerful computers, abundant and very high quality consumer goods, and devices able to cure most diseases by repairing the body from the molecular level up.[6]

Other scientists and organizations are more cautious, some suggesting that we are unlikely to experience any such thing, at least in our lifetime. But who knows what a nano world could hold in store for our grandchildren? If, as IMM Senior Research Fellow Ralph Merkle asserts, 'many of the material dreams of humanity can be fulfilled'[7] by molecular nanotechnology, then let us dream: what might molecular manufacturing mean for fashion?

...flights of nanofashion fancy

If matter can be designed and assembled at the molecular level into almost any structure or shape, then 'nano-mastery' of materials could open up entirely new possibilities. Take carbon, for example: silk, cotton, rubber and kevlar are all made from carbon — it just depends on how we arrange the molecules as to whether it becomes hard or soft, stiff or stretchy. Fashions could also be created from unconventional materials, such as pearl or gold. Why wear imitation when you can have the real thing? Let's start by replacing all those boring old diamante and plastic crystals, beads and sequins with pearls made to 'self-assemble', or form themselves into a soft, silky pearl cloth. Wondering what to wear to the Christmas party? Simply load a gold-particle assembly programme from your favourite designer into your nanofashion compiler to create the ultimate real gold frock.

Once we have overcome the initial excitement of creating the most impossibly expensive dress ever made, what else might we desire? How about losing all the discomforts in fashion but upping the 'wow' factor? Imagine vertiginous stilettos that

231
The Numerical Aerospace Simulation Systems Division of the NASA Ames Research Center, Moffett Field, California is conducting research into the molecular-sized devices in nanotechnology. This image depicts designs for two fullerene nanogears with multiple teeth. The hope is that one day products can be constructed of thousands of tiny machines that could self-repair and adapt to the environment in which they exist.

232
In his 1998 exhibition 'Issey Miyake: Making Things' at the Cartier Foundation in Paris, Miyake presented a series of clothes which seemed to emerge like a butterfly from a chrysalis. Using his 'starburst' technique, three-dimensional garments of cotton, flannel, wool, felt or jersey were heat-pressed with a membrane of metallic foil and then magically extracted from a thin two-dimensional wafer. Miyake has celebrated technology throughout his career in a quest to offer us new visions of what clothes might be. In future, nanotechnology could present us with entirely new ways of thinking about making fashion.

189

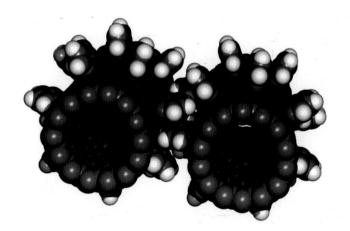

231
NASA
Fullerene nanogears

232
Issey Miyake
Making Things, 1998

233
Walter Dorwin Teague
Nearly Nude evening dress, 1939

massage the balls of your feet or wrap your foot with all the comfort of a cosy slipper. While we are in the land of fairytales, let's make it a stretchy glass slipper. Assuming by this stage that we will also be able to replicate DNA from extinct organisms, and that ethically this is no longer an issue, give me a fur coat made from woolly mammoth. Exotic animal furs could be farmed without the animals. Computing cashmere cardigans, which fluff up and cling tightly when you are chilly, might also brush your skin gently with your favourite moisturising perfume. In fact, all the visions discussed in this book would be accomplished overnight, combined in one garment that you re-configure at will.

Fashion, in this distant world, becomes something akin to designer DNA, a ribbon of atomic instructions that tells assemblers, the new couture workroom *petites mains*, how to organize a bunch of molecules. The fashion designer becomes a conductor of couture chemistry.

...the celebrity tablet

There's one slight snag with this ultra-luxurious new nano-wardrobe – its wearer. What is the point of all this spectacular glamour on a wrinkly, sick old body? In a world that permits bits to be reorganized at will, we are more likely to be preoccupied with what we look like than worried about what to wear. Research into nanomedicine will no doubt spin off into the highly lucrative global cosmetic industry – the concerns of ageing long forgotten, replaced instead by aesthetic beauty adjustments. Nanocosmetics could make you up molecularly. A cream might apply cosmetic nanomachines topically, reorganizing cells to give a different skin tone, or you could swallow a tablet for blond hair. Hair, face and body could be transformed by millions of nanomachines that race around seeking out cells to modify.

233
Walter Dorwin Teague believed that universal heating and air-conditioning meant that women would not expect clothes of the future to keep them warm or cool. Instead, 'Women of the future...will have beautiful bodies...gowns will be designed to reveal the beauty of their bodies and will afford only the minimum of covering that will accentuate their attractiveness... materials will be of chemical origin, and many will be either transparent or translucent, with an individual life of their own.' Autonomous fabrics that adjust their structure or chemistry might be possible in a nanofashion future.

234
In the 1960s, at the Lady Jane boutique on London's Carnaby Street, an in-store artist painted 'clothes' directly onto a client's skin. Nanotechnology may lead to paintable fabrics that self-assemble into garments.

191

234
Paint-on clothing, 1960s

Body treatments may go beyond altering the surface structure. Following a nano-beauty programme might enable anyone who could afford it to re-shape their face and body into their dream of perfection. If unsure as to what suits you, you might choose to try-on someone else: become a Kate Moss or Brad Pitt look-alike. Perhaps in the same way people aspire to certain fashion brands and designers today, there might be trends for wearing celebrity identities. In the future, you might spot a dozen versions of the same star walking down the street. Clothes, hair and make-up may differ – these could be options offered when you choose the programme. Nicole Kidman doppelgangers might be glimpsed at a party, one glamorously attired version chatting to another sporting jeans and a T-shirt, while the actress herself is having a quiet evening at home. Instead of wearing the same lip colour as a particular actress in a movie, you could wear the actress's face. Max Factor, creator of make-up looks for the stars, might supply the external appearance of stars *as make-up*. Getting the celebrity look may simply be a matter of consuming a capsule.

...fashioning the future

Have we entered the world of science fiction or are we glimpsing fashion of the twenty-second century? On one level at least, molecular manufacturing seems to offer environmental rewards: products could be broken down and reassembled, making it the definitive recycling technology. Long before we reach this stage, however, people will demand reassurance from scientists that adequate controls are in place. The potential creation of so-called 'gray goo', self-replicating nanorobots that convert the natural world into more copies of themselves, is a major concern in the nanotech community. As Drexler notes in *Engines of Creation*, 'The gray goo threat makes one thing perfectly clear: we cannot afford certain kinds of accidents with replicating assemblers.'[8]

235/236
Tim Fonseca is a science fiction computer-graphics illustrator who visualizes nanotechnology concepts. These images are based on projections by Robert Freitas in his book *Nanomedicine*. They picture several billion dermal display nanorobots residing in the epidermis of a human hand that can be used as a display screen to access real-time physiological information or other stored data. Dermal nanorobots might also be used aesthetically for full-motion animation (skin video) or with subdermal nanospeakers – 'talking tattoos'.

237
In future, if you don't have time to get to the hairdressers, Tim Fonseca imagines you might employ flying saucer 'barberbots'. You would make a choice from a selection of pre-set hairstyles and programme the barberbots to perform their magic.

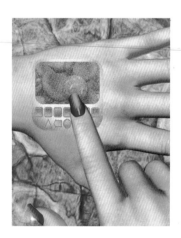

235
Tim Fonseca
Dermal display

236
Tim Fonseca
Dermal display

237
Tim Fonseca
Barber saucers

Much hype and speculation currently surrounds the business side of nanotechnology, with many companies eagerly laying claim to being nano-enterprises. The nano-prefix simply means that their work takes place within the uppermost nanometre scale. The electronics industry mostly still operates in a micro-world, building *micro-electromechanical machines* (MEMs) that are thousands of times larger than the proposed nanomachines.

In 2002, the US Army invested $50 million in a major new research centre, located at MIT, called the Institute for Soldier Nanotechnologies (ISN), with the aim of creating a 'twenty-first century battlesuit'. Their vision is one of 'a bullet-proof jumpsuit, no thicker than ordinary spandex, that monitors health, eases injuries, communicates automatically, and maybe even lends superhuman abilities.'[9] In the short term this research targets military uniforms, but no doubt in the long term any nanotech breakthroughs will be transferred to sportswear and, eventually, fashion.

In 2004, the European Commission valued global investment in nanotechnology at five billion euros.[10] And in the 1996 book, *Nanotechnology: Molecular Speculations on Global Abundance*, B.C. Crandall forecast that in the twenty-first century 'molecular engineering will emerge as a multitrillion dollar industry that will dominate the economic and ecological fabric of our lives'.[11] As for trying to predict what nanotechnology might hold in store for fashion, it is too early to say. We don't yet know what questions to ask. In a utopia of abundance and aesthetic perfection for all, will fashion itself become extinct? What will define creativity, exclusivity, rarity and luxury if potentially everyone can have them? If external appearance is in a state of constant flux, even more so than today, might we be forced to focus on the person within? As fashion travels into the future will we be wearing material or machine? Or will fashion,

238
A fanciful image depicts mobile nanorobotic cleaners (green) patrolling the lungs, collecting inhaled debris and transporting it to recycling stations (blue-grey).

239
Another imagined *in vivo* operation where nanorobots clean fatty deposits from the inside wall of a diseased artery.

238
Tim Fonseca
Lung cleaners

239
Tim Fonseca
Artery cleaners

changing from moment to moment, become mere entertainment, nothing more than a passing construct? Guests could leave a fashion show wearing entirely different outfits to those in which they arrived; mimicking molecules could allow fashion editors to 're-organize' their own clothes, copying the new look they have viewed just seconds earlier. Ultimately, the question may not be '*what* is fashion?' but '*when* is fashion?'

240/241

In Alexander Mackendrick's dark Ealing comedy of 1951 Alec Guinness played Sidney Stratton, a man who invents a miraculous fabric that does not get dirty or wear out. What initially seems like a blessing for mankind is not viewed so by the garment manufacturers, who try to suppress it. After all, once someone buys one of his suits they will not ever have to wash it or buy another, and the clothing industry would collapse. A warning perhaps that not all new technologies are welcomed and anything that has the potential to put many people out of work will meet with severe resistance.

194

240
The Man in the White Suit, 1951

240
The Man in the White Suit, 1951

Chapter 1

1 Kamitsis, *Paco Rabanne* (1996), p. 65.

2 Ibid., p. 90.

3 The 'mono-material' culture promotes the manufacture of products from one material source in order to assist disassembly and recycling. Fleeces made by Patagonia, for example, use cloth, labels and zips that are all made from one polyester source – recycled plastic bottles – making the recycling process straightforward.

4 Miyake and Fujiwara, *A-POC Making*, p. 68.

5 Author interview with Manel Torres, December 2003.

6 Ibid.

7 Ibid.

8 Ibid.

Chapter 2

1 See Bradley Rhodes, 'A brief history of wearable computing': www.media.mit.edu/wearables/lizzy/timeline.html

2 Arnold Schwarzenegger starred in the 1984 film as the *Terminator*, a human-looking cyborg who has data overlaid on his vision of the world.

3 M. Weiser, 'The Computer for the Twenty-First Century', *Scientific American*, September 1991, pp. 94–100: www.ubiq.com/hypertext/weiser/SciAmDraft3.html

4 Marzano et al., *New Nomads*, p. 7.

5 Swade, *The Difference Engine*, p. 166.

6 See E. R. Post, M. Orth, P. R. Russo, N. Gershenfeld, 'E-broidery: Design and fabrication of textile-based computing': www.research.ibm.com/journal/sj/393/part3/post.html

7 See P. J. Massey, 'Fabric Antennas for mobile telephony integrated within clothing': www.ee.ucl.ac.uk/lcs/papers2000/lcs030.pdf

8 See M. Bickerton, 'Effects of fibre interactions on conductivity, within a knitted fabric stretch sensor', Proceedings of IEE Eurowearble Conference, 2003, pp. 67–72.

9 See 'Intrabody Signalling': www.media.mit.edu/physics/projects/pan/pan.html

10 US Patent 6,754,472 was issued to Microsoft, 22 June 2004, for a 'method and apparatus for transmitting power and data using the human body.'

11 See thermogenerator at Infineon: www.infineon.com/cgi/ecrm.dll/jsp/showfront end.do?lang=EN&channel_oid=-11511

12 See work by Nathan S. Schenk and Joe Paradiso at MIT: www.media.mit.edu/resenv/power.html

Chapter 3

1 Cunera Buijs and Jarich Oosten (eds), *Braving The Cold: Continuity and Change in Arctic Clothing*, Leiden, 1997, p. 18.

2 Miyake and Fujiwara, *A-POC Making*, p. 71.

3 See Fritz Vollrath and David P. Knight, 'Liquid Crystalline Spinning of Spider Silk', *Nature*, 410, 29 March 2001, pp. 541–8.

4 See Spinox press release: www.isis-innovation.com/about/news/spinox.html

5 Dr Fowler's paper 'Development of Bio-Active Fabrics' can be found at: www.mne.umassd.edu/faculty/alexbio.html%20

6 Author interview with Dr David Hepworth, August 2004.

7 Author interview with Tobie Kerridge, August 2004.

8 Ibid.

9 TC&A manifesto is at: www.tca.uwa.edu.au/atGlance/glanceMainFrames.html

10 www.knowear.net

Chapter 4

1 See The Art Guys with Todd Oldham, '*Suits: The Clothes Make the Man*', New York, 2000. In the 'Suits' project the Art Guys (Jack Massing and Michael Galbreth) sold advertising space on their suits to corporate clients.

2 www.lunar.com/portfolio/client_archive/blu.html

3 Ibid.

4 Author interview with Maggie Orth, February 2004.

5 Ibid.

6 Also cited are James Bond's invisible car in *Die Another Day*, directed by Lee Tamahori, 2002, and Harry Potter's invisibility cloak.

7 See James Owen, 'Militaries Study Animals for Cutting-Edge Camouflage', *National Geographic News*, 12 March, 2003: http://news.nationalgeographic.com/news/2003/03/0311_030312_secretweapons1.html

8 Rivers, *The Shining Cloth*, p. 59.

9 See Richard V. Gregory, Timothy Hanks, Robert J. Samuels, 'Dynamic Color Change Chameleon Fiber Systems – The Next Step', Richard V. Gregory, Timothy Hanks, Robert J. Samuels: www.ntcresearch.org/pdfrpts/Bref0602/M01-CL07-02.pdf

10 See Stephen S. Hardaker and Richard V. Gregory, 'Progress toward Dynamic Color-Responsive 'Chameleon' Fiber Systems', *MRS Bulletin*, 28, no.8, August 2003:www.mrs.org/publications/bulletin/2003/aug/aug03_abstract_hardaker.html

Chapter 5

1 Rivers, *The Shining Cloth*, p. 56.

2 Author interview with Hussein Chalayan, May 2004.

3 *C* magazine, 1 September 2002.

4 Pavitt, *Brilliant*, p112.

5 Julie Wosk, *Women and the Machine: Representations from the Spinning Wheel to the Electronic Age*, Baltimore and London, 2001; p. 73.

6 Ibid., p. 74.

7 Linda Hales, 'Furnishings That Blossom With Whimsy', *Washington Post*, 31 May 2003, p. C.02.

8 Author interview with Despina Papadopoulos, February 2004.

9 Ibid.

10 Author interview with Elise Co, February 2004.

11 See 'Development of Bio-Active Fabrics': www.mne.umassd.edu/faculty/alexbio.html%20

Chapter 6

1 Bolton, *The Supermodern Wardrobe*.

2 Stern, *Against Fashion*, p. 32.

3 See J. Lahann et al., 'Reversible Switching of Surfaces', *Science*, 299, 371, 2003.

4 See Karen Lurie, 'Instant Armour': www.sciencentral.com/articles/view.php3?article_id=218392121&language=english

5 See Yoseph Bar-Cohen, 'Transition of EAP material from novelty to practical applications – are we there yet?': ndeaa.jpl.nasa.gov/ndeaa-pub/SPIE-2001/Paper-SPIE-4329-02-Applications.pdf

Chapter 7

1 *Rapid Prototyping* falls into two main categories: additive and reductive. In the first, layers of material are deposited onto a substrate and bonded thermally using a laser or glue; in the second, a substance such as resin or starch is sculpted into shape by cutting away material to produce a finished object.

2 Author interview with Philip Delamore, April 2004.

3 Author interview with Suran Goonatilake, July 2004.

4 A Japanese technique of dyeing cloth to create a decorative pattern.

5 Author interview with Philip Delamore, April 2004.

6 Ibid.

Chapter 8

1 See J. Rantanen et al., 'Smart Clothing for the Arctic Environment', *Proceedings of the Fourth International Symposium on Wearable Computers*, October 2000, pp. 15–23.

2 For an example of an anti-bacterial fabric treatment, see 'Purista': www.purista.co.uk

3 For an example of an anti-UV fabric treatment, see 'Ciba® TINOSORB®': www.cibasc.com/index/ind-index/ind-home_fab/ind-hfc-uv-absorbers.html

4 For an example of an anti-static fabric, see 'X-static': www.noblefiber.com

5 See Ros Picard's Affective Computing Group at MIT: http://affect.media.mit.edu and www.bartneck.de/link/affective_portal.html

6 Author interview with Adam Whiton, November 2004.

7 Ibid.

8 Ibid.

9 Arizona State University professors Frederic Zenhausern and Ghassan Jabbour displayed a prototype 'Scentsory Chameleon Bodysuit' at NextFest 2004. This military outfit included sensors that could 'sniff' the air for chemical or biological agents; low temperature fuel cells would provide a lightweight power source for a soldier's equipment; and a flexible electroluminescent display wrapped onto the cuff to give the soldier updated commands, warnings and other information.

Chapter 9

1 E-textiles and actuating fabrics are also discussed in chapters 2 and 6.

2 www.francetelecom.com/en/financials/journalists/press_releases/CP_old/cp040701.html

3 See Chapter 4.

4 www.psfk.com/2004/09/is_that_a_mobil.html

5 Blum, *Shocking!: The Art and Fashion of Elsa Schiaparelli*, p. 208.

6 Author interview with Paul Gough, March 2004.

7 See www.isi.edu/stories/34.html

Chapter 10

1 Stephenson, *The Diamond Age*, p. 35.

2 Feynman's talk is published online: www.zyvex.com/nanotech/feynman.html

3 Philip E. Ross, 'The Road To Lilliput', *Nanotech*, 99, 15 June & 1 July, 2001, p. 48.

4 The term nanotechnology was first coined in 1974 by Norio Taniguchi, a researcher at the University of Tokyo, who used it to refer to the ability to engineer materials precisely at the nanometre level. See: www.nanotec.org.uk/finalReport.html

5 *Unbounding the Future* is published online: www.foresight.org/UTF/Unbound_LBW/chapt_7.html, scroll down to 'Smart Cloth'.

6 www.imm.org

7 Ralph C. Merkle, 'Nanotechnology: Why People Care (or: Thinking Outside the Dot)': www.foresight.org/NanoRev/Ralph Merkle.html

8 *Engines of Creation* is published online: www.foresight.org/EOC/EOC_Chapter_11.html, see 'The Threat From The Machines'

9 http://web.mit.edu/isn/aboutisn/index.html

10 The Royal Society and the Royal Academy of Engineering, *Nanoscience and Nanotechnologies: Opportunities and Uncertainties*, London, 2004, Chapter 1: www.nanotec.org.uk/finalReport.htm

11 Crandall (ed.), *Nanotechnology*, p. 2.

NOTES

Actuator
A mechanism that puts something into automatic action, originally referring to an engineering component, but now used in reference to fibres and fabrics that might be electronically or chemically triggered to change shape or otherwise respond to a stimulus.

Ambient intelligence
Describes technologies that combine ubiquitous computing and intelligent systems to create electronic environments that are sensitive and responsive to people, putting humans at the centre of technological developments.

Augmented reality
Combines a real scene with a virtual scene as generated by a computer, such that the viewer perceives a single enhanced reality.

Bioactive
Any substance that has an effect on living tissue can be said to be bioactive.

Bioluminescence
Light produced by a chemical reaction that takes place within certain creatures, e.g. the firefly.

Biometrics
Biometrics are automated methods of recognizing a person based on a physiological or behavioural characteristic, e.g. facial shape, the retina of the eye or voice pattern. Biometric data can also refer to the measurement of body systems such as heart rate and respiration.

Biomimicry
The imitation of biological designs, processes and laws in order to solve human problems, e.g. a solar cell inspired by a leaf.

Bioreactor
A large vessel for growing micro-organisms.

Biotechnology
The means to manipulate organisms to provide desirable products for man's use.

Bluetooth
The specification for wireless communication that allows devices such as mobile phones and PDAs to exchange data. Named after Harald Bluetooth, a mid-tenth century Danish king who united Denmark and Norway.

Chameleon camouflage
Created by matching the object to be camouflaged to its background colours, rendering it virtually invisible to the eye. Conceptually, this is the same process as that used by the chameleon.

Chemiluminescence
Light produced by the release of energy from a chemical reaction.

Computer-aided design and manufacture (CAD/CAM)
The use of computers in designing a product and in controlling its manufacture.

EFAB
The EFABTM process, developed by Mircrofabrica Inc., can generate extremely complex, truly 3D microdevices by depositing many tens of precision metal layers. This will make microtechnology accessible to mainstream applications in a wide range of industries.

Electroluminescence
A technology used to produce a very thin display screen, as deployed in some portable computers: an electric current is passed through a grid of wires that lie between plates coated with a phosphorescent substance, emitting points of light known as pixels.

Electroactive polymers (EAPs)
EAPs are useful in biomimetic applications, such as the creation of artificial muscles for robotic systems, and potentially also in fibres for responsive, smart fabrics.

Electrochromism
An electrically generated reversible colour change causing alteration in the absorption or reflection of light through a material.

Electro-rheostatic materials (ER)
Fluids that can change consistency from thick to nearly solid within a millisecond when exposed to a magnetic or electric field.

Electroluminescence
The conversion of electrical energy into light in a liquid or solid substance, by means other than heat.

Electro-textiles (e-textiles)
The use of yarns that can transmit electrical signals or current to create woven or knitted fabrics that have conductive properties.

Ferromagnetic fluid
Fluids with properties, including density, that change in the presence of an electromagnetic field.

Flexible displays
Computer screens that are almost as portable, lightweight and easy to read as paper, and can be used to a create a changeable display.

Global Positioning System (GPS)
A worldwide radio-navigation system using a network of satellites which allows a user with a handheld device to calculate their global position accurate to a matter of metres.

Haptics
Derived from the Greek word to grasp or touch, this is the science of applying tactile sensation to human interaction with computers. Haptic interfaces combine computer software and hardware to give and receive information in the form of a felt sensation on some part of the body.

Infrared
Refers to a type of wireless connection commonly used on laptop computers and devices such as mobile phones and PDAs. Uses light from the non-visible part of the spectrum to beam data over short distances, but needs to have clear line-of-sight between devices to work.

Light-emitting diode (LED)
Light-emitting diodes are like tiny lightbulbs; they use minimal electricity and generate relatively little heat, making them suitable for incorporating into textiles and clothing. Widely used to create illuminated displays and in electronic devices as status lights.

Magneto-rheological materials (MR)
See Electro-rheostatic materials and Ferromagnetic fluid.

Materials science
The study and practical application of any of the following: metals, ceramics, polymers (plastics), semiconductors, and combinations of materials called composites.

Micro-electromechanical machines (MEMs)
Microscopic machines, often smaller than a grain of sand, composed of switches, gears, motors, mirrors, pivots, and optical and electrical components, on a chip a few microns to millimetres across.

Molecular manufacturing, molecular nanotechnology
A type of manufacturing technology that will be achievable once things can be built at the atomic or molecular level, with every atom in a specified place. So, a nanofactory will create a diamond structure to fill a specified volume by rearranging matter with atomic precision instead of a shape being created by cutting a block of material or carving out a mold.

Multimedia messaging service (MMS)
The ability to send messages comprising a combination of text, sounds, images and video to MMS-capable mobile phone handsets.

Nanotechnology See Molecular manufacturing

Nitinol (Nickel Titanium Naval Ordnance Laboratory)
The generic name for the family of nickel-titanium alloys is Nitinol. See also Shape memory.

Organic light-emitting diode (OLED) and Polymeric light-emitting diode (PLED)
Unlike LCD screens, which require backlighting, OLED and PLED displays are emissive devices: they emit light rather than modulate transmitted or reflected light. OLED is beginning to replace LCD technology in handheld devices such as PDAs and cellular phones because the technology requires less power, offers higher contrast and is cheaper to manufacture, and the newer PLED screens are cheaper and consume even less power.

Personal area network (PAN) & body area network (BAN)
The use of the electrical conductivity of the body and/or garments as a data network for the exchange of digital information between wearable devices.

Phase change material (PCM)
A 'latent' thermal storage material that uses chemical bonds to store and release heat. PCMs are generally solid at room temperature but as they absorb more heat they change in state or 'phase' and liquefy, cooling the surrounding area. When the ambient temperature in the space around the PCM drops, it solidifies, releasing its stored latent heat. PCMs absorb and emit heat while maintaining a nearly constant temperature themselves.

Photoluminescence
The property of a material that enables it to emit light for a period after a source of light energy has been directed at it, such as materials that glow in the dark after being exposed to light during the day.

Photovoltaic
A material capable of producing an electrical current from light.

Photonic band-gap fibre
PBG is an energy range (and corresponding wavelength range) where a material neither absorbs light nor allows light propagation. The energy gap in a PBG material can ideally be closed by means of inducing defects. Such doping or even switching will allow light of the forbidden energies to pass through the material in controllable ways, thus these materials have potential applications ranging from optical communications to quantum computation.

Photoluminescence
Describes the property of a material to emit light for a period of time after a source of light energy has been directed at it.

GLOSSARY

Materials that glow in the dark after being exposed to light during the day are an example of this.

Piezoelectric materials (PZT)

Materials that create an electrical charge when mechanically stressed, e.g. squeezed or squashed. Among the natural materials with this property are quartz, certain polymer films and human skin.

Polymer

A natural or synthetic substance made of many relatively simple repeating chemical units or molecules, e.g. starch or Perspex.

Rapid manufacture 3DP (3D Print)

A rapid prototyping process developed at MIT. Layers of powder are formed by an inkjet printer to build up a 3D component. The term is sometimes used generically as a synonym for rapid prototyping.

Rapid prototyping

Term used to describe those technologies that additively 'grow' a design in order to produce a 3D component or object. Processes used in Rapid Prototyping include Stereolithography (SLA), Object 3D printing, Laminated Object Manufacture (LOM), Fused Deposition Modelling (FDM) and Selective Laser Sintering (SLS).

Radio-frequency identification (RFID)

A system designed to carry information in tiny mobile transponders known as tags. These discrete tags can inform on the location of goods in transit, the location of and details about people and the location/stage of an item in a manufacturing line.

Sensor

Sensors are electric transducers that translate a physical property such as humidity, heat or light into an electrical signal, e.g. thermostats (which control temperature). By connecting a variety of sensors through short-range wireless connections, sensors will develop into complex networks that will enable people to control more of the physical world.

Shape memory

The property of some materials that enables them, when deformed, to return to their original shape through the application of heat. Materials include certain alloys, polymers and gels.

Smart system (active smart, passive smart)

Materials that respond to differences in their environment (e.g. temperature, light) and respond to those conditions by changing in some way. Smart materials appear to 'think' and can exhibit 'memory' as they revert back to their original state.

Teledildonics

Teledildonics is a virtual-reality application that allows users to have interactive sex with other users who may be a great distance away. While eventually technology will allow for full-body suits that stimulate all five senses, the first generation of teledildonic devices are much simpler.

Thermochromism

A reversible change of colour that occurs due to a change in temperature. Takes place in certain dyes made from liquid crystals.

3Dimensional printing, 3D manufacture

see Rapid prototyping

Tissue engineering

A field that brings together biology, materials science and biomedical engineering with the goal of long-term repair and replacement of failing human tissues and organs.

Transgenics

The production of organisms that contain altered genes from other organisms. It allows scientists to develop organisms that express a novel trait not normally found in the host species.

Ubiquitous computing

Ubiquitous computing is the third wave in computing, now just beginning. Initially, there were mainframe computers, shared by lots of people. Now we are in the personal computing era: one person, one computer. The next stage is ubiquitous computing, or the age of calm technology, when technology will recede into the background of our lives – one person, many invisible computers embedded in everyday objects.

Wireless networking

Refers to technology that enables two or more computers to communicate using standard network protocols, but without any network cables. Any technology that does this could be called wireless networking, however it generally refers to wireless Local Area Network (LAN) that uses a specific industry standard called IEEE 802.11.

GLOSSARY

General

www.azom.com
A–Z guide to materials

www.inteletex.com
Latest news on textiles and technology

www.futurephysical.org
Body and technology

www.invista.com
Invista

www.materialconnexion.com
Commercial materials research resource

www.iom3.org
Institute of Materials

www.qinetiq.com
British Defence Laboratory

www.eurekalert.org
US science news

www.esa.int/export/esaCP/ESARDG2VMOC
index_0.html
European Space Agency (ESA), smart textiles
technology transfer

http://hub.interaction-ivrea.it/resources/000338
Interaction Design Institute, Ivrea

www.studio-creatif.com/Gb/Vet/Vet01
Concept01Fr.htm
France Télécom

www.showstudio.com
ShowStudio, fashion research projects online

http://avantex.messefrankfurt.com
Avantex, biennial exhibition and symposium
for future apparel textiles

www.waltervanbeirendonck.com
Walter Van Beirendonck

www.alexandermcqueen.net
Alexander McQueen

1 The Spray-On Dress

www.fabricanltd.com
Fabrican

www.pierrecardin.com
Pierre Cardin

www.pacorabanne.com
Paco Rabanne

www.isseymiyake.com
Issey Miyake

www.shimaseiki.co.jp/homee.html
Shima Seiki 3D knitting machines

2 The Programmable Jacket

www.wearcam.org
Steve Mann

http://eyetap.org
Personal imaging, Steve Mann's research group
at University of Toronto

www.media.mit.edu/wearables/lizzy/
timeline.html
History of wearable computing

www.natick.army.mil
US Army Soldier Systems Center, Natick

www.foster-miller.com/t_s_electro_textiles.htm
Foster-Miller e-textiles

www.xybernaut.com
Xybernaut

http://physics.ucsc.edu/people/eudaemons/
layout.html
Eudaemons shoe computer

www.parc.xerox.com
Xerox PARC

www.research.philips.com/technologies/
misc/homelab
Philips HomeLab

www.infineon.com
Infineon Technologies

www.electronicshadow.com/mediacol/veste/
concepteng.htm
Communicating scarf

www.eleksen.com
Eleksen

www.media.mit.edu/physics/projects/
pan/pan.html
MIT, Personal Area Networks (PAN)

www.almaden.ibm.com/cs/user/
pan/pan.html
IBM, Personal Area Networks (PAN)

http://ttt.media.mit.edu/index.html
MIT, Things That Think

www.media.mit.edu/hyperins/levis
MIT, musical jacket

www.media.mit.edu/wearables
MIT, wearable computing

http://web.media.mit.edu/~rehmi/fabric
Early experiments in smart fabric or 'washable
computing'

www.scottevest.com
Scottevest

http://composite.about.com/library/PR/2001/
blustuttgart1.htm
Photovoltaic fabric

www.wearablegroup.org
Carnegie Mellon University wearables

www.ece.cmu.edu/~etex
Carnegie Mellon University e-textiles

www.research.ibm.com/journal/sj/393/part3/
post.html
E-broidery

www.wearable.ethz.ch
ETH Zurich wearable computing lab

http://wearables.cs.bris.ac.uk/index.htm
Bristol wearable computing project

www.cc.gatech.edu/ccg/wear/index.html
Georgia Tech wearables

www.bekaert.com/bft/Products/Innovative
%20textiles/Key%20applications/Intelligent
%20textiles.htm
Bekaert conductive yarns

www.redwoodhouse.com/wearable
Wearable computing resource and links

www.ideo.com/mit/index.html
MIT & IDEO Digimoda wearable computing
project

3 The Growable Suit

www.xs4all.nl/~ednieuw/Spiders/InfoNed/
webthread.html
Spider silk

www.arachnology.org/Arachnology/Pages/
Silk.html
Spider silk links

www.isis-innovation.com/spinout/
spinox.html
Spinox

www.nexiabiotech.com
Nexia Biotechnologies, BioSteel

www.ntcresearch.org/pdf-rpts/AnRp03/
M00-MD03-A3.pdf
Bioactive fabrics

www.speedo.com
Speedo

www.fujibo.co.jp/us/chitopoly/chito
_01.html
Chitopoly

www.crabyon.it
Crabyon

www.artsadmin.co.uk/artists/ah/photo
synthesistext.html
Heather Ackroyd and Dan Harvey

www.lifegem.com
LifeGem

www.biojewellery.com
Biojewellery

www1.imperial.ac.uk/medicine/about/
divisions/is/tissue
Imperial College tissue engineering

www.tissue-engineering.net
Tissue engineering

www.tca.uwa.edu.au
The Tissue Culture & Art Project

www.knowear.net
KnoWear

www.biomimicry.net
Biomimetics

www.rdg.ac.uk/Biomim
University of Reading biomimetics

www.bath.ac.uk/mech-eng/biomimetics
University of Bath biomimetics

4 The Invisible Coat

www.lunar.com
Lunar Design

www.pioneer.co.jp
Pioneer

www.ifmachines.com
International Fashion Machines

www.interactivecolors.com
Chromatic inks

www.eink.com
E-ink

www.rle.mit.edu/rleatmit/2003february
article01.htm
Yoel Fink, MIT

www.ntcresearch.org/pdf-rpts/Bref0604/
M01-CL07-04e.pdf
Chameleon fibres

http://projects.star.t.u-tokyo.ac.jp/projects/
MEDIA/xv/oc.html
Susumu Tachi's transparency cloak

www.cdltd.co.uk/technology/200.asp
Cambridge Display Technology

www.universaldisplay.com
Universal Display

5 The Glowing Ballgown

www.alexandermcqueen.net
Alexander McQueen

www.meta-design.jp/k1space11.html
Erina Kashihara

www.glowmania-international.com
Photoluminescent materials

www.superbrightleds.com
LEDs

http://shop.dotlight.de
LEDs

www.5050ltd.com
5050

www.mintymonkey.com
Elise Co

200

WEBSITES

http://acg.media.mit.edu/people/elise/glow/
index.html
Elise Co raincoat

http://acg.media.mit.edu/people/elise/
thesis/index.html
Elise Co thesis

www.loop.ph
Rachel Wingfield

www.elwirecheap.com
EL wire

www.beingseen.com
Electroluminescent materials

www.elumin8.com
Electroluminescent systems

www.ntcresearch.org/pdf-rpts/AnRp03/
M00-MD03-A3.pdf
Bioactive fabrics

www.lifesci.ucsb.edu/~biolum
Bioluminescence

www.luminex.it
Luminex

6 The Shape-Shifting Skirt

www.designinsite.dk/htmsider/
md950.htm
Smart materials resource

www.designinsite.dk/htmsider/
inspmat.htm
Smart materials information and demos

www.corponove.it
Corpo Nove

www.gzespace.com
Grado Zero Espace

www.diaplex.com
Shape memory polyurethane

www.cpcompany.com
CP Company

http://web.mit.edu/isn/people/faculty/
mckinley.html
Gareth McKinley, MIT

www.autexrj.org/No4-2003/0078.PDF
Electroactive fabric research

http://ndeaa.jpl.nasa.gov/nasande/lommas/
eap/EAP-web.htm
Electroactive polymers (EAPs)

www.cutecircuit.com
Cute Circuit

7 The Instant Bikini

www.dsmsomos.com/pressroom/
press_releases/2002/somos2002-02
crowrn/en/somos02-2002-crownen.htm
Marcel Wanders's project

www.freedomofcreation.com
Freedom of Creation

www.pacorabanne.com
Paco Rabanne

www.cadcamnet.com
CAD/CAM

www.cc.utah.edu/~asn8200/rapid.html
Rapid prototyping

www.bathsheba.com
Bathsheba Grossman, rapid prototyping
artist

www.materialise.com
Materialise

www.zcorp.com
Z Corp

www.bodymetrics.com
Bodymetrics

8 The Caring Camisole

www.aspenaerogel.com
Aerogel products

www.corponove.it
Corpo Nove

www.gzespace.com
Grado Zero Espace

www.esa.int
European Space Agency

www.gorix.com
Gorix

www.thenorthface.com
The North Face

www.clothingplus.fi
Finnish wearable technology

www.tut.fi/index.cfm?MainSel=-1&Sel
=1680&Show=1568&Siteid=32
Tampere University of Technology, Finland

www.intelligenttextiles.com
Woven electronic textile developers

www.sensatex.com
Sensatex

www.gtwm.gatech.edu
Georgia Tech Wearable Motherboard

www.vivometrics.com
Vivometrics

www.verhaert.com
Verhaert, Mamagoose

www.bodymedia.com
BodyMedia

www.hitair.co.uk
Hit Air

www.no-contact.com
No-Contact Jacket

www.extremetech.com/slideshow/0,2394,
l=&s=25500&a=133422,00.asp
Siggraph Cyberfashion Show 2004

www.karrysafe.com/home.html
Karrysafe

9 The Talking T-Shirt

http://home.snafu.de/maubrey
Benoît Maubrey, electronic clothing projects

www.e2senneville.com
Elisabeth de Senneville

www.studio-creatif.com/Vet/Vet03Create
Wear02Fr.htm
France Télécom

www.xslabs.net/intimate.html
Joey Berzowska

www.smartsecondskin.com/main/
smartsecondskindress.htm
Jenny Tillotson

www.design.philips.com/about/design/
section-13480/index.html
Levi's-Philips ICD+

www.nike-philips.com
Nike-Philips

www.softswitch.co.uk
Softswitch

www.canesis.com
Textile technology research

www.eleksen.com
Eleksen

www.gorix.com
Gorix

www.burton.com
Burton

www.infineon.com/hub
O'Neill-Infineon

www.5050ltd.com
5050

www.autexrj.org/No4-2003/0078.PDF
Electroactive fabric research

www.cutecircuit.com
Cute Circuit

www.fashionvictims.org
Fashion Victims

www.ideo.com/portfolio/re.asp?x=50165
IDEO technojewelry

www.ices.cmu.edu/design/streetware/
strwrechoose.html
Carnegie Mellon accessories project

www.smartextiles.co.uk
Central Saint Martins Smart Textile Network

www.wlic.ac.uk/research/research.asp
UMIST smart textiles research

http://a.parsons.edu/~alison/thesis
Alison Lewis, touch clothes

http://kingkong.me.berkeley.edu/~nota/
research/TactileVestPaper.htm
Tactile Vest project

10 The Self-Assembling Raincoat

www.zyvex.com/nanotech/feynman.html
Feynman talk transcript

www.nano-tex.com
Nano-Tex

www.nano-sphere.ch
Schoeller NanoSphere

www.ntcresearch.org/pdf-rpts/Bref0604/
M03-CL07s-04e.pdf
Carbon nanotube e-textile research

www.foresight.org
Foresight Institute

www.nano.org.uk/index.html
Institute of Nanotechnology

www.azonano.com
Nanotech resource

www.imm.org
Institute of Molecular Manufacturing

www.ewels.info/img/science
Nanotech image gallery

www.nanomedicine.com/NMI.htm
Robert Freitas, *Nanomedicine* book online

web.mit.edu/isn
MIT Institute for Soldier Nanotechnologies

WEBSITES

Bar-Cohen, Yoseph (ed.)
*Electroactive Polymer (EAP) Actuators
as Artificial Muscles: Reality, Potential, and
Challenges* (Bellingham, WA, 2001)

Barfield, Woodrow and Thomas Caudell (eds)
*Fundamentals of Wearable Computers
and Augmented Reality* (New York, 2001)

Bass, Thomas A.
The Eudaemonic Pie (Boston, 1985)

Benaim, Laurence
Issey Miyake (Fashion Memoir) (London,
1997)

Blum, Dilys E.
*Shocking!: The Art and Fashion of Elsa
Schiaparelli* (New Haven and London, 2003)

Bolton, Andrew
The Supermodern Wardrobe (London, 2002)

Braddock, Sarah E. and Marie O'Mahony
*SportsTech: Revolutionary Fabrics,
Fashion and Design* (London, 2002)

—, *Techno Textiles: Revolutionary
Fabrics for Fashion and Design*
(London, 1999)

Crandall, B. C. (ed.)
*Nanotechnology: Molecular
Speculations on Global Abundance*
(Cambridge, MA, 1996)

Crispolti, Enrico
Il Futurismo e La Moda, Balla e gli altri
(Venice, 1986)

Drexler, K. Eric
Engines of Creation (New York, 1986)

— and Chris Peterson
*Unbounding the Future: Nanotechnology
Revolution* (London, 1992)

Dunne, Anthony
*Hertzian Tales: Electronic Products,
Aesthetic Experience and Critical Design*
(London, 1999)

— and Fiona Raby
*Design Noir: the Secret Life of Electronic
Objects* (Basel and London, 2001)

Evans, Caroline
Fashion at the Edge (New Haven and
London, 2003)

—, Suzy Menkes, Ted Polhemus and
Bradley Quinn,
Hussein Chalayan (Rotterdam, 2005)

Frankel, Felice and George Whitesides
*On the Surface of Things: Images
of the Extraordinary in Science*
(San Francisco, 1997)

Freitas, Robert A.
Nanomedicine: Basic Capabilities
(Georgetown, TX, 1999)

Gershenfeld, Neil
When Things Start to Think
(New York and London, 1999)

Gray, Chris Hables (ed.)
The Cyborg Handbook (London, 1995)

Handley, Susannah
Nylon: The Manmade Fashion Revolution
(London, 1999)

Hibbert, Ros
*Textile Innovation: Interactive, Contemporary
and Traditional Materials* (London, 2004)

IEEE Computer Society
*Third International Symposium on Wearable
Computers, Digest of Papers*
(San Francisco, 1999)

Kalman, Tibor and Maria
(un)Fashion (London and New York, 2000)

Kamitsis, Lydia
Paco Rabanne (Paris, 1996)

—, *Paco Rabanne (Fashion Memoir)*
(London, Rotterdam, 2001)

Mendes, Valerie
Pierre Cardin: Past, Present, Future
(London, 1990)

Miyake, Issey and Dai Fujiwara
A-POC Making (Vitra Design Museum,
Weil-am-Rhein, 2001)

Moffitt, Peggy and William Claxton
The Rudi Gernreich Book
(New York, 1991)

Morrison, Philip and Phylis
Powers of Ten (New York, 1983)

Musée Galliéra
Mutations Mode: 1960–2000
(Paris, 2000)

Myerson, Jeremy
IDEO: Masters of Innovation
(London, 2001)

Negroponte, Nicholas
Being Digital (New York, 1995)

Norman, Donald A.
The Invisible Computer
(Cambridge, MA, 1998)

—, *Emotional Design*
(Cambridge, MA, 2004)

Pavitt, Jane
Brilliant: Lights & Lighting (London, 2004)

Plant, Sadie
*Zeros & Ones: Digital Women
& the New Technoculture*
(London and New York, 1997)

Quinn, Bradley
Techno Fashion (Oxford, 2002)

Rivers, Victoria Z.
*The Shining Cloth: Dress & Adornment
that Glitters* (London, 1999)

Sato, Kazuko and Hervé Chandes
Issey Miyake: Making Things (Paris, 1999)

Stephenson, Neal
The Diamond Age (London and
New York, 1995)

Stern, Radu
Against Fashion: Clothing as Art 1850–1930
(Cambridge, MA, 2003)

Swade, Doron
*The Difference Engine: Charles Babbage
and the Quest to Build the First Computer,*
(London and New York, 2001)

Tao, Xiaoming (ed.)
Smart Fibres, Fabrics and Clothing
(London, 2001)

Van Beirendonck, Walter
Mutilate: An Artist's Book (Gent, 1997)

Watkins, Susan M.
Clothing, The Portable Environment
(Ames, IA, 1984)

Wosk, Julie
*Women and The Machine:
Representations from the Spinning
Wheel to the Electronic Age,*
(Baltimore and London, 2003)

Zolli, Andrew (ed.)
*TechTV's Catalog of Tomorrow:
Trends Shaping Your Future*
(Indianapolis, 2002)

BIBLIOGRAPHY

So many people helped to bring this project to fruition. Foremostly, I am grateful to Caroline Evans, Reader in Fashion and Director of the Fashion & Modernity Research Project at Central Saint Martins College of Art & Design, University of the Arts London, for her wisdom and the encouragement to turn my research into a book. The book was produced with assistance from the Fashion & Modernity Research Project, funded by the Arts and Humanities Research Council (AHRC). At Central Saint Martins, I am very grateful to Jane Rapley, Dean of Fashion & Textiles for her enthusiasm and support, and to Peter Close for his help in administering the many complexities of this project. I am indebted to Marketa Uhlirova in so many ways – she enriched the picture research, bringing historical context to the discussion together with insightful comments and criticism. Lei Yang rescued me at a critical time to handle additional picture research with the utmost professionalism. Marketa, Caroline Evans and Rebecca Lowthorpe contributed greatly to the text, reading drafts and helping to structure and edit. Dr David Hepworth gave generously of his time and patience as a scientific advisor. At The Studio, it was a delight to work with Nicole Stillman, who was conscientious and good humoured. Thank you to James and Angela at VinMag Archive, Shannon Bell and all the designers, artists, scientists, companies and institutions who contributed essential imagery, interviews and expertise.

A big thank you to Leonie and ARM for all their production and communication support throughout the entire project. My utmost thanks to everyone at Thames & Hudson for realizing the project. Love and thanks to Ian, Bec, Bean, Sam, Hamish and Hugle, who, though frantically busy with their own creative lives, supported me in mine. Finally, my greatest debt of all is to Warren and Nick, I am touched by their generosity, enthusiasm and belief – their rare magic turned the dreams into realities.

Supported by

 Arts & Humanities Research Council

We would warmly like to thank all those who gave their time, expertise and enthusiasm to the fashion shoots:

Art direction and photography: Warren du Preez and Nick Thornton Jones
Styling: Suzanne Lee assisted by Sam Perry
Photographic and production team: Giles Price, Algernon Brinton, Nicole Stillman
Specialist light: Chris Levine, technical production and assistance by Ram Malocca
Hair: Raphael Salley at Streeters (thanks to Paula at Streeters) and Dejan Cekanovic
Make-up: Tanya Chianale at The Worx assisted by Vimala Clark.

Casting by Sarah McManus:
Clara Benjamin (with thanks to Giorgina at Take 2)
Irina and Melody (with thanks to Noelle at Storm)
Lisa Ratliffe and Carolyn Park at Select (with thanks to Mandy at Select)
Madelaine Hjort, Jagna and Viktoria S (with thanks to IMG)
Karolina Malinowska, Candice Lake (with thanks to Versae at Next)

The 3D images were created with the expert assistance of:
Kevin Stenning at Rapido3D
Jim Bowers at Journeyman
Special thanks to Hector McLeod and Pete Reilly at GLASSWORKS London for their craftsmanship, support and vision.

The author and publishers acknowledge the following sources of quotations reproduced in this book on the pages listed.

p. 13 Paco Rabanne: Lydia Kamitsis, *Paco Rabanne*, Editions Michel Lafon, 1996
p. 25 Rudi Gernreich: Peggy Moffit and William Claxton, *The Rudi Gernreich Book*, Rizzoli, 1991
p. 41 Neil Gershenfeld, *When Things Start to Think*, Hodder and Stoughton, 1999
p. 59 Issey Miyake: Issey Miyake and Dai Fujiwara, *A-POC Making*, Vitra Design Museum, 2001
p. 147 Raymond Loewy, 'Fashions of the Future', American *Vogue*, February 1939, Condé Nast Publications
p. 165 Sonia Delaunay: Radu Stern, *Against Fashion*, MIT Press, 2003
p. 183 Neal Stephenson, *The Diamond Age*, Viking, 1995

ACKNOWLEDGMENTS

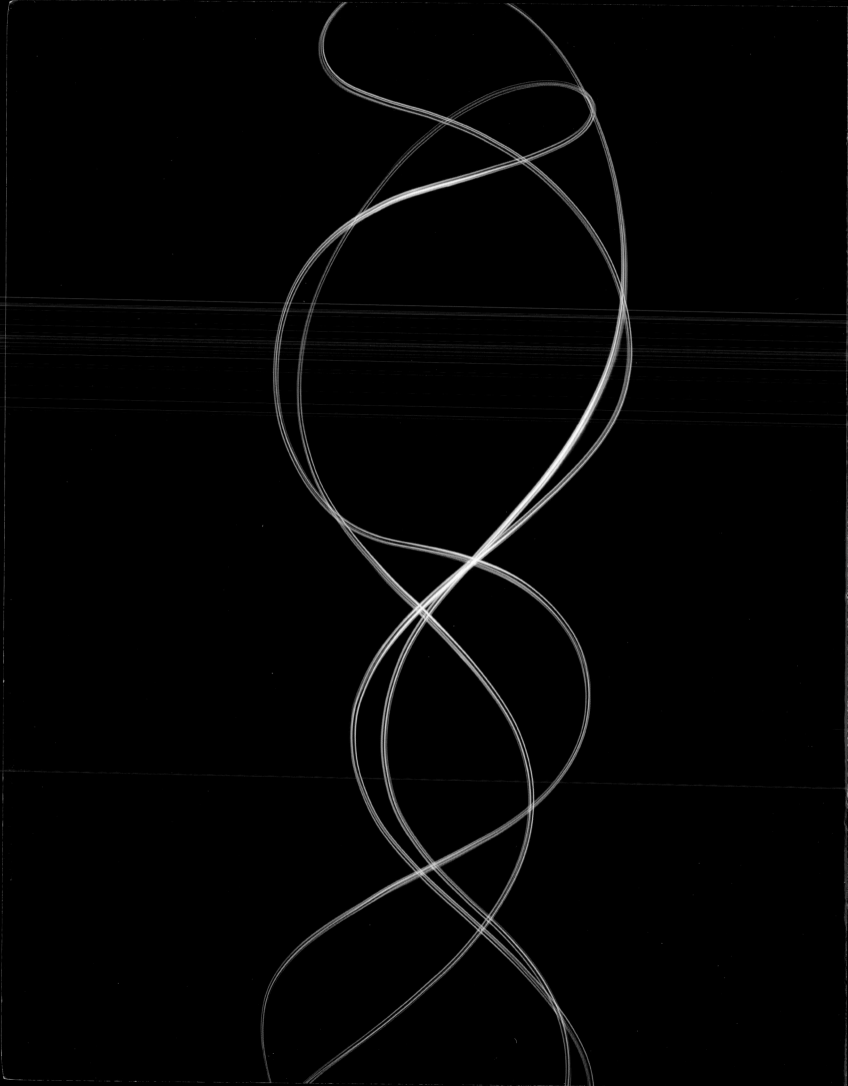

PICTURE CREDITS

INDEX

INDEX